MW01690708

Bertha D. Winston

UNSHAKABLE FAITH

Hello Sarah,

I promised when the book was published I would mail you a copy. It's here and I hope you enjoy the stories of all these phenomenal. Thank you for all of your help & support. May God bless and keep you.

UNSHAKABLE FAITH

REDIRECT, REDEFINE & RENEW YOU

ALLISON G. DANIELS

AGD Publishing
Upper Marlboro, Maryland

AGD Publishing Services

Printed in the United States of America

Paperback ISBN: 978-1-7372867-8-3
Ebook ISBN: 978-1-7372867-8-3

For details, Email: allisongdaniels@verizon.net
Or visit us at www.allisongdaniels.com

Visionary: Allison G. Daniels
Cover Design:
Interior Layout: Tywebbin Creations
Editor: Sheila Hightower

TABLE OF CONTENTS

FOREWORD

As a relationship coach and professional speaker, I see so many people who are discouraged by the trials of life and oftentimes struggling with their faith, specifically while in the midst of their challenges, so I am happy to see Visionary Allison Daniels bring light to the power of faith. Allison is an esteemed writer who is often providing a platform for others to share their stories of overcoming temptations, trials, and difficult circumstances.

Each story is relatable, and I found myself encouraged by the individuals' strengths and transparencies. We all have found ourselves, at one point or another, in situations where our faith was both challenged and tested. "Unshakable Faith" invites the reader to go on a journey of strong faith and relentless hope. With everything that is going on in the world today, this could not be a better time for all of us to reach down deep and grab faith by the hands. Now is the time for all of us to stand firm on our beliefs with complete confidence and reliance that with faith and our trust in God, all things are possible.

The entire Christian life is lived out on the foundation of faith. This Book will shine light on the fact that God is trustworthy, and He honors His promises. It is our faith in God that makes us certain of these things. God has provided a better way for us all by way of faith. As you read each testimony, may a steadfast faith rise up within you so much, that you will believe and know that with assuredness, God has an outcome just as beneficial as the trial is hard. May faith be your fuel as you continue your walk of life!

Warm Regards,

Temesha Siler-McNeill
Innovative Leader and Coach
CEO of TSM Training Services, LLC
Certified Green Belt Six Sigma Leader

JAMES 1:2-4

"Count it all joy, my brothers, when you meet trials of various kinds, for you know that the testing of your faith produces steadfastness. And let steadfastness have its full effect, that you may be perfect and complete, lacking in nothing."

INTRODUCTION

In Unshakable Faith: These stories are from women who (are indeed, pearls of great price) who have encountered trials and tribulations that challenged their faith, but you will see that their faith was indeed, "Unshakable".

Minister Allison G. Daniels and several other women have shared stories from the heart as to how they had to redirect their emotions, redefine who God said they were, and their journey of being renewed, thus, allowing God to make a victorious difference in their lives, all to His glory

In this Book Unshakable Faith, your journey of wholeness will begin with the power, the praise, and the presence of the Lord. This Book will challenge you to take back your life and enable you to walk in your authority so that you can face tomorrow – today.

REFINING (REFINER'S) FIRE

Temesha Siler-McNeill

Owner and CEO of TSM Training Services, LLC.
Certified Green Belt Six Sigma Leader
A certified relationship coach

ABOUT THE AUTHOR

Temesha Siler-McNeill is a disciplined, innovative leader and coach with over 25 years of corporate management experience. She is the owner and CEO of TSM Training Services, LLC. Temesha is a certified Green Belt Six Sigma Leader, with extensive training in project management, leader development and organized management. Temesha is also a certified relationship coach. She spends her time coaching individuals and training couples to not just survive but thrive.

Temesha works hard to help leaders, couples, and business owners to successfully maximize their time, manage conflicts, create goals, enhance their brand, and find purpose that will sustain growth and long-term survival. She provides group coaching and one-on-one coaching sessions where she focuses on building confidence, self-motivation and living with purpose.

Temesha enjoys speaking at conferences, leadership seminars, churches, and community events. You can catch her often delivering and presenting training workshops to corporations and the community while communicating her greatest passion, inspiring and motivating individuals to act with HOPE. The McNeill

Family are the Founders of The Family Rocks Foundation, INC, which is a non-profit, strictly dedicated to strengthening families with training seminars, conferences, and retreats. While she is striving to be a world changer daily as a Christian, Author, Entrepreneur, and Philanthropist, her most important role is that of wife and a mother to her two children. Temesha's enthusiasm for life will, without a doubt, motivate anyone into action. Temesha Siler-McNeill has answered the call to educate, empower, and inspire others by giving away her "gifts and talents" to everyone she encounters.

REFINING (REFINER'S) FIRE

The year was 2019. It was just two weeks before Christmas and I was at work when a coworker noticed that my neck was swollen. I had not noticed the swelling earlier that morning, so I was shocked when I immediately looked in the mirror, which by now was later in the afternoon and I saw the swelling. I instantly knew that something was wrong. I immediately called my doctor, and I was able to get an appointment to see him the same day. At the time, I had no idea that this day would be the beginning –the first day of many more appointments. My doctor scheduled me for a CT scan and later, a biopsy. The first biopsy was inconclusive, so my doctor recommended surgery to get a better concrete (reliable) sample. I will never forget that surgery because it was December 31, 2019, when family, friends and everyone were preparing for New Year's Eve celebrations, I was preparing for surgery.

Well, the results from the biopsy did not come back in my favor. I later had a PET scan which revealed multiple areas within my neck that carried cancerous cells. I was then assigned to an Oncologist who diagnosed me with Stage II, Non-Hodgkin's Lymphoma. Lymphoma is a complicated cancer which begins within infectious-fighting cells of the immune system, called lymphocytes.

The lymphocytes are present in the lymph nodes. The cancer was found in my neck and chest lymph nodes. I was informed that my treatment would be six months of twelve rounds of chemotherapy. Upon hearing this news, I felt numb, shocked and it was as though I was outside of my body. All types of things went through my mind. It was the start to my survival journey and the only thing I was certain of was that I needed God!

This situation allowed me to present an unveiled face to the Lord our God. I began to take off my fake mask of strength and unwavering courage. I started to cry out to my Heavenly Father as I took the position as His daughter. The position of His daughter allowed me to be open and with complete honesty to God, that I feared chemotherapy. I was fearful of the unknown. I didn't know what I was supposed to do, what to expect, and I felt hopeless. I knew in my heart that I needed my Father and my Savior. I remember lying before the Lord and just crying. This was my very first step to healing because this was the moment my walls came tumbling down, just like the walls of Jericho. In this moment, I fully, wholehearted surrendered, and my heart found comfort in the arms of my Heavenly Father. I immediately felt loved, safe and at peace. It was this moment that my Father let me know He was fighting for me! God reminded me of what HE said in His Word in Exodus 14:14 to the children of Israel. God said He would fight for me in my silence. Now, when

I look back on this encounter, God responded to me in the same way I would respond as an earthly parent if one of my children were in the same situation. I would wrap them in my arms, kiss away their tears and reassure them, Mommy is fighting for you!

I didn't feel the need to talk about cancer. I didn't want to give cancer any power with my words. I felt the desire to talk more about God and His promises and His power. I refused to let cancer outshine God. Even when I refused to give power to cancer, the enemy would try to use others around me. They were fearful of cancer and seemingly bowed down to cancer. During those times I would pray with them to the Most-High God. Praising God for His goodness and counting this situation as joy. My friends and family were taken aback by this and often said that they felt a sense of peace afterwards. The faith they saw had nothing to do with a feeling but everything to do with a promise, — His promise to me. I didn't know what the result would be, but I knew that God was fighting for me and that gave me peace. Because God doesn't lose and because God can't lose! It doesn't matter what you see with the naked worldly eye, hear me when I say –God doesn't lose!!

During this time, I could feel God calling me to be more, to trust more and to allow the Holy Spirit to comfort me, lead me and guide me toward healing. To surrender! The

Lord was ushering me into a healing that was bigger than that of my body which was being attacked by cancer. The Lord let me know HE wanted to heal my soul. Healing of my soul began with forgiveness.

My heart was hurting for a couple of different reasons. I had not forgiven those who I thought had taken advantage of my kindness, mishandled my heart and betrayed my trust. In my mind, I was justified for giving those people the silent treatment and the cold shoulder. I mean after all, I was hurt. Isn't that what we do, in that we justify our actions! Nevertheless, God revealed to me, and I finally realized, I can be guilty of not dealing with conflict and disagreements quickly. I will never forget when God revealed to me about this pain in my heart. I knew the pain was real, but I never allowed myself to be vulnerable enough to feel the pain. I needed to accept my own responsibility in the situation. God showed me that I didn't trust Him to protect and heal my heart. I had a hard time crying to my Heavenly Father when I was hurt. And an even harder time crying in front of others when I felt pain. As this was being revealed to me, I knew the moment had come for me to reach out to individuals and ask for their forgiveness of me and to release my forgiveness toward them. I then reached out to some people and started the cleansing process of forgiveness. I cried, they cried, and the journey of healing my soul was taking a step in the right direction. I was able to take this step because I truly trusted God with my broken heart and my unresolved pain. I was confident that God wanted to give me total and complete healing. That healing started with my soul before the healing process of my body.

God put me in a place where I could not be prideful nor insecure. This was the time that God needed me most to shine light upon Him, His Word, His promises and to have FAITH. I'm not saying I didn't have rough days, challenging circumstances, and some days of wavering faith. What I am saying is that God made every day with Him better than any other day elsewhere. My relationship with my Heavenly Father went to a brand-new level, and I made a choice to accept the challenge as Job did, which is one of the most popular stories found in the Bible. I declared that I would come out as pure gold. I realized that God wanted me to be more vulnerable with Him. God wants us all to be in a place of surrender to Him because this is where He shines the brightest. I now understand why I wasn't vulnerable with others over the years. I had never truly been vulnerable with my Father in Heaven. Vulnerability means you can be your true self and not be afraid of hurt, judgment, pain, or shame. I have prayed to God all my life and received an abundance of love and gifts from God. However, when it came to being vulnerable, I suppressed those feelings and would keep it moving. I viewed it as a sign of strength. I now know that true strength is found in vulnerability. If you find yourself unable to allow others to see your pain, to see you cry and see you struggle, then ask yourself why? A part of that discovery process might reveal to you that you have not truly surrendered to God. Because surrendering to God means I have full trust in God and the process. Giving God my tears and pain is my way of saying Jesus take the wheel! Jesus is a better driver, and the map belongs to Him anyway. I am a passenger along for the ride and I have FAITH that I will arrive at the destination God desires for me.

I have strong faith, but not because of a good feeling. I have strong faith because of what I know. I know what God says in His Word about me and who He is to me. I know that God is compassionate, loving and kind toward us. That God loves me and you so much that He gave His only begotten son to die for our sins. I know that God will never leave us nor forsake us! I know that He has plans to prosper us and not to harm us. I know that all things work together

for the good of those who love God. I could go on and on about what I know!! And because of what I know, I have a strong faith in the Lord our God. The fire that was meant to burn me, is the same fire God used to refine me.

Heart Surgery Leads to Strong Faith

(Thistlebend Ministries)

QUESTIONS TO PONDER

Would you be willing to ask the Lord to search your heart today?

Would you be willing to ask Him to reveal areas of sin in your thinking, in your heart, and in your life?

Would you be willing to ask Him to show you any actions, words, or deeds that indicate any unrighteousness?

PRAYER

Dear God, hear my prayer. O LORD give ear to my pleas for mercy! In your faithfulness answer me in your righteousness, in Jesus' name. Amen!

"Hear my prayer, O Lord; give ear to my pleas for mercy! In your faithfulness answer me, in your righteousness!" Psalm 143:1, ESV

I'M STILL STANDING

Tamala Jenise Coleman

Founder and Editor and Chief of NSpire Christian Magazine.

ABOUT THE AUTHOR

Tamala Jenise Coleman is a 3x best-selling author with 11 books published.

Tamala has been writing for over 16 years and she has developed the potential to write, intentionally, to encourage and inspire others. Also, Tamala has her credits as a director and producer of stage plays and film. To date, Tamala has won several film-script credits. Tamala is also the Founder and Editor and Chief of NSpire Christian Magazine. Tamala strives to empower women and inspire the masses with the power of faith.

Tamala is also a member of "Women with Wings, International" where she is on the Board of Directors. This foundation is Christian based and assists women who have been entrapped in Domestic Violence and Sex Trafficking. Tamala has also hosted a number of Podcasts for 6 years. To name a few "Spiritually Speaking" on AMFM247 Broadcasting Radio Show; "Amazing Grace" on TalkZone Radio where she interviews Ministers, Authors, Business Owners, and just everyday people with a testimony to share with the world and share the Good News of Jesus Christ. Tamala is currently a part of the Network "KPTV" (Kingdom Purpose TV) where she delivers a Spiritual Word once a week. She is also a part of Elite Conversations Marketing where she delivers the Motivational Audio Podcast "WOW" twice a month. Tamala is the recipient of several awards: Radio Personality of the Year (ACHI Magazine Awards 2019); "Women Rocking the Web Awards" 2022; Writer's Magazine Cover Page Feature; ATL Magazine and she has received many more accomplishments and accolades, which are too many to name herein.

Tamala worships devotedly with New Springfield Missionary Baptist Church for over 40 years and she serves as a Sunday School Teacher.

Tamala is a loving and devoted wife to Brian Coleman and mother to their three wonderful children, Thaddeus, Tiffanie, and Brianna.

Social Media Contacts:

- Facebook: Tamala Coleman
- Instagram: Iam_TamalaColeman
- www.TamalaColemanbooks@ yolasite com
- www.nspirechristianmagazine.com

I'M STILL STANDING

"Therefore whoever hears these sayings of Mine, and does them, I will liken him to a wise man who built his house on the rock: and the rain descended, the floods came, and the winds blew and beat on that house; and it did not fall, for it was founded on the rock." –Matthew 7:24-24

In the above Scripture, Jesus tells us of the wise man who chose to build his house on the rock –rock solid, steady, and true foundation. He could have chosen a more convenient foundation that would crumble under pressure, or be moved by the wind, but he chose a strong foundation that would not waver in a storm. Just like this wise man, you must take care to build your life on the true, unshakable foundation, the Word of God! The English Dictionary's definition of unshakable means someone's trust or belief is unshakable; it is firm and cannot be made weaker or destroyed: *She was blessed with an unshakable belief in her own abilities; to not be weakened.* I have learned that the Word of God is the only foundation that will never fail, change, or pass away. Many people spend so much of their lives waiting for happiness or waiting for retirement years to find out that they are empty and unfulfilled.

Ephesians 2:10 says, "For we are His workmanship,

created in Christ Jesus for good works, which God prepared beforehand that we should walk in them." God has prepared good works for us to accomplish! He has a plan for each one of us that requires so much more than the simple pursuit of pleasure, and when we choose to build our house on the Rock, we will have righteousness, peace, and joy in the Kingdom of God.

Many believers are of the mindset that they need only to be good enough, kind enough, or spiritual enough to be right with God. Some may even think they are saved simply because they believe God exists. But you can only be made right with Him through Jesus who is the way, the truth, and the life. In John 14, Jesus tells us that no one can come to the Father except through Him. We also need to understand that God cares so deeply for us that He wants to be a part of our *daily* lives. He does not want us to hope that we are behaving well enough or doing enough good deeds to make up for our mistakes. As He shows us in His Word, the only way to be made righteous is through faith in Jesus.

Faith grows upon a solid foundation. God loves us just the way we are, but He does not, and He will not leave us the way we are; our faith is meant to grow and become stronger throughout our life's journey, especially the Christian journey.

In 2 Thessalonians 1:3 Paul writes, "We ought always to

thank God for you, brothers, and sisters, and rightly so, because your faith is growing more and more, and the love all of you have for one another is increasing." (NIV).

We are not designed to only exist on a foundation, but to continuously build upon our faith as we walk with God. As we grow on this journey, we must remain steadfast and unmovable. In my life I have endured much, and I have overcome much, and I must say, that if it had not been for my faith in God, I would have given up a long time ago. I am sure I am not alone; many of us are walking on grounds that eventually would have swallowed us up or we may have fallen deep into an abyss, but due to our faith, we are still standing and walking on a strong foundation of God's Word and His promises.

There is a song Bishop Paul S. Morton sings that I love very much, and it states:

I'm still standing,

I'm still trusting

I'm still holding on to what I believe

Still motivated

Fully persuaded

I'm still standing

Standing on the Word

On the Word that's in my heart.

Your Word says I am healed

So that means I am healed

Your Word says I am free

So that means I am free

Your Word says I am

More than a conqueror

Through Jesus

Standing, standing

Standing on the promises

Of Christ my Savior

Standing, standing

Standing on the promises of God.

These words state just how we should stand in our faith, and we must have an unshakable faith, even when things around us are falling to pieces. I can say and I declare that I am still standing on the Word that holds me; the Word that heals me, the Word that frees me and the Word that has kept me through it all.

I'm STILL STANDING and TRUSTING in God and standing on His promises!

You may be going through trying times right now, or maybe you feel like you are at a stand-still in your life and you just don't know how you are going to make it. Yes, God has a word for you –for your soul. You are an overcomer and I encourage you to hold on to your faith. Pray and seek God. No matter how hard it gets hold on to unshakable faith. I am reminded of the familiar Scripture in

Hebrews 11, "Now faith is the substance of things hoped for, the evidence of things not seen."

Throughout my life as a believer, I have come to depend on this Scripture as an encouragement. Why? Because throughout my life I had to realize that without faith I have nothing; without my faith I am nothing. Honestly, I would have lost my mind. Yet, God has kept me through my many tests and trials, challenges, and tribulations. As a podcast host for the past three years I have had the opportunity to speak with both women and men who were guests on my shows and many shared their life's journey with me –the good, the bad, and the ugly, and as I listened to their sharing, I had to count my blessings because I felt that my life was worthless and that I had endured some things that I never shared with anyone, yet perfect strangers unapologetically shared their intense life stories with me and the world through my podcast.

So, I am sharing this testimony with you because many of us are not true to ourselves, because the reality is that we all have a testimony, and we all have a past. Your experiences may not be my experiences, your testimony is not my testimony, however, we all have testimonies, and they are not just for us, but for others who need to know that they too can have this unshakable faith and they too can stand, even in the midst of their situation.

This unshakable faith to stand, even in the hardest times, can seem lonely sometimes; it can even feel exhausting, especially if you are trying to stand on the Word of God.

Hebrews 11:16 states "But now they desire a better, that is, a heavenly country. Therefore God is not ashamed to be called their God, for He has prepared a city for them." (KJV)

Faith is the substance or the guarantee that those things which you are waiting for will come to pass. Faith is the evidence we can have when we cannot see the manifestation. Faith begins when you drown your doubts, cast off fear and anchor in the Truth of God's Word. God is a rewarder of those who diligently seek

Him. If you believe that you are not experiencing His grace or the deliverance you need, seek Him. I refuse to allow anyone, or anything to stand between me and faith and my trust in God. So, as you read these words, I pray that you too will stand on your faith. Stand, therefore! Stand and know that God will never leave you nor forsake you.

In Ephesians 6:13-17, it says "Therefore take up the whole armor of God, that you may be able to withstand in the evil day, and having done all, to stand. Stand therefore, having girded your waist with truth, having put on the breastplate of righteousness, and having shod your feet with the preparation of the gospel of peace; above all, taking the shield of faith with which you will be able to quench all the fiery darts of the wicked one. And take the helmet of salvation, and the sword of the Spirit, which is the word of God;" (NKJV)

It takes faith and God's grace to follow God's plan for our lives. God is the Author and the Finisher of our faith. Taking the chance to step out of your comfort zone and walk in faith, is what it is all about; that's where the miracle happens because moving in the direction of uncharted waters in your life can be very scary, but praying to God helps to establish that relationship with Him and as you grow in Him, as you delight yourself in Him, He will give you the desires of your heart. We must understand that faith always means risk. Everything in life is a risk.

Ecclesiastes 10:8 says, "He who digs a pit will fall into it, And whoever breaks through a wall will be bitten by a serpent. He who quarries stones may be hurt by them, And he who splits wood may be endangered by it."

There's nothing we can do that doesn't have some element of risks or taking chances, if you will, in or with it. But the greatest risk of all is how we relate to other people and how we relate to God in doing something about those relationships.

Mark 12:30 says, "And you shall love the Lord your God with all your heart, with all your soul, with all your mind, and with all your strength.' This is the first commandment."

You take a risk when you love with all your heart. Is it worth it? Absolutely! Especially loving God with all your heart. When I think about my husband and how I love him and he loves me, we both took risks in a new relationship, not knowing if it would work or not. Yet, after 17 years I can truly say it was worth it. We would not have known it if I had not taken the risk.

Jesus reminded us that one of the greatest mistakes we can make is to play it safe with our lives. He said, "If you try to keep your life for yourself, you'll lose it." True scripture! Faith is stepping out and doing what God has asked you to do when you can't see what will happen in the end. You don't know exactly what God is going to do in the end, but you know He's asking you to step out in faith. I can remember when I finally made the decision to write my first book; I realized I couldn't keep talking the good talk –that with all sincerity, I was gonna do it; I had to make a move toward writing the book. I had to pick up a pen and write something down; I had to start the book.

Talk is cheap until you make a move. So, I encourage you to step out in faith; lean on God's unchanging hand and believe God for that unshakable faith, and, oh, keep standing!

PRAYER

Heavenly Father, teach us to lean on Your Word and trust Your Word. God, give us Your strength to hold on, even in trying circumstances and difficult times. Help us God to stand always on Your promises and have the unshakable faith that only You alone can give. We trust You, and we give You all the honor, the praise and the glory, in Jesus' name. Amen!

REJECTION IS RE-DIRECTION

Gizelle Taylor-Daniels

Clinical Office Manager
Best-Selling and International Author

ABOUT THE AUTHOR

Deacon Gizelle Taylor-Daniels is the wife of Jermaine Daniels, a mother of two, and grandmother of two. She is a Clinical Office Manager with the Family Medical Counseling Service, Inc. (FMCS), Pediatrics Department. Gizelle is a Best-Selling Author, and an International Author. Gizelle is also a contributing author in Visionary Author Reverend Allison G. Daniel's Anthology: Empowered to Win.

Gizelle is genuinely enthusiastic about helping individuals achieve ultimate health care. She is committed to the promotion of preventive pediatric care as well as to the promotion of physical, mental, and the social wellbeing of children with the aim of attaining optimal health.

Gizelle is inspired by a very memorable quote: "My mission in life is not merely to survive, but to thrive; and to do so with some passion, some compassion, some humor, and some style." –*Maya Angelou*

Gizelle holds a B.A. with honors in Health Services and a Certificate as a Community Health Worker from Trinity Washington University.

REJECTION IS RE-DIRECTION

OVERCOMING THE EMOTIONAL PAIN OF REJECTION

The voice of this chapter will be from one who was in need of healing –a voice of healing. A voice that had to turn unto God for peace, spiritual peace from a society that is full of lingering social problems such as rejection. Rejection can be hard to live with whether it is from a relationship, work, or other life challenges/issues of life. Although rejection generated a strong and negative emotion within me, I learned that rejection was not necessarily a terrible thing. That is because there is a positive phrase to keep in mind if ever rejected, and that is: "Rejection is Re-Direction and Re-Protection." Contrary to what one may believe, sometimes rejection is for our own good. Although rejection may not always be protection, protection will be the outcome if we trust God to order our steps. He will always protect us. Romans 8:28 (KJV) says, "And we know that all things work together for good to those who love God, to those who are called according to His purpose."

Rejection has a way of not only impacting our emotional well-being, but it can also damage our mood and self-esteem. Rejection caused my sense of belonging to become unstable. Consciously and unconsciously, I became isolated from people, places, and events. I began to realize that I had become emotionally wounded, secondary to rejection. My wounds were invisible to the naked eye, however, the emotional scarring from the pain of rejection had begun to determine the quality of my life as an adult. This very feeling caused me to reflect and acknowledge my earliest experience of rejection. I was forced to face the childhood rejection of the absence of my birth father. The rejection of my birth father was an emotional and hurtful feeling a pain that lingered into my adulthood. Although I was adopted, I was raised by an incredible man who had chosen me, and fathered me, and proudly called me his daughter. However, the rejection of my birth father was very profound and prevalent. From my earliest childhood experience of rejection, a mask began to develop as a form of protection against the heart-breaking feelings which were also connected to triggers of feeling under-valued by individuals.

While I was rejected, both verbally and physically by my birth father, I received Agape love from my Heavenly Father, as well as my adoptive father. God's faithfulness and His Agape love provided and protected me with a father who loved me as his own. Studying the Word of God taught me how to accept the rejection of my birth father and how to love him, still. I also had to forgive my birth father. I realized the faith that I was operating in was an unshakable faith. Most individuals do not grow stronger when everything is working for them, but when we are forced to cope with the unexpected and or the undesirables of life, we must not be shaken. Psalm 62:1-2 (NIV) says, "My soul finds rest in God alone; my salvation comes from him. He alone is my rock and my salvation; he is my fortress; I will never be shaken." I was able to see the strength of my faith during my emotional responses to rejection.

I may have been detained in bondage secondary to rejection, but I was not denied. God used every source of pain, suffering and rejection to raise me up and above, and to grow stronger with the ability to walk and operate in unshakable faith. Also, my experience with rejection has caused quite a stir with awareness. I have such a desire to have influence in the lives of others, and especially those who have and are experiencing rejection. Herein, I want to articulate the importance of rejection and how it is mistakenly identified. Often individuals overlook and label rejection as sensitivity. Rejection is a spirit –one of the most common tools the devil uses to destroy who we were created to be and our purpose in life. John 10:10 (KJV) says, "The thief cometh not, but for to steal, and to kill, and to destroy I am come that they might have life, and that they might have it more abundantly." I could not control the choice of others and their decision to inflict pain upon me, however, I was able to take control of the damage and the pain that developed within me. I began to assess the damage, I accepted the reality, and asked God to help me. I no longer looked at rejection in the same negative manner. Instead, I replaced rejection with re-direction allowing my Heavenly Father to order my steps to the Balm in Gilead.

SHOW THYSELF APPROVED

Hello!!! Allow me to introduce myself. I am Gizelle Taylor-Daniels, and I am created in the image of God. Genesis 1:27 (NIV) says, – So God created mankind in his own image, in the image God, he created them; male and female he created them. Psalm 139:14 (KJV) says, I will praise thee, for I am fearfully and wonderfully made marvellous are thy works; and that my soul right well. I am not defined by my past triggers of rejection. I have risen-up and out against the battles in my mind and the pain that once resided in my heart. The yoke of oppression, the yoke of bondage, and the yoke of rejection no longer lives within me. I have an anointing over my life and God has blessed and empowered me to heal the brokenhearted. I am Salt and Light, an influencer to those who are in bondage, to those who are hurting, and to those who are unwavering. I am valuable, I am free, and I am redeemed. I will continue to experience God's faithfulness. I will no longer tarry I will keep my trust in Him. I decree and declare a legacy of UNSHAKABLE

FAITH for future generations. My life will be of excellence and integrity. I will stand firm, steadfast, resolute, unwavering, bent but not broken, stretched and strengthened in my faith walk with God!!

I survived the storms of adversity secondary to my foundation. I cried out asking God to heal me and provide me peace. My wounds became my strongholds which attracted negative and difficult circumstances to my life. I did not desire a foundation of negativity, that is, not believing in myself, doubting my self-esteem, and or operating through life in anger instead of faith. Instead, I desired peace, hope, and faith in God, and unshakable faith. When your faith is built on the right foundation, you can face life's problems from the smallest to the greatest without being shaken. But when your faith does not exist, you will buckle at the knees and struggle when difficult circumstances come your way. We must secure a solid foundation. When you put your faith in God as your foundation for your life rather than putting it in family, friends, yourself, your work, or anything else, God will give you His peace.

Through God's Word I was able to gain strength in my faith. I wanted that strong type of faith described in the story of Shadrach, Meshach, and Abednego in the Book of Daniel. I wanted to navigate life in faith without any doubt knowing that God will deliver me from the pain that felt like the heat from the flames of fire. Once I became a willing participant trusting the process and doing the work, I was empowered with God's strength. I continued to gain strength but this time I was also able to overcome the stronghold of rejection. Acknowledging my identity, which is the anointed, fearfully and wonderfully made marvelous Gizelle. God's strength is empowering!!

Here is a gentle reminder, when you find yourself facing adversity, difficulty in relationships, and you lack peace, unshakable faith has nothing to do with your personal strength; it is the strength of God that matters. Every pain serves a greater purpose in our lives. Every failure leads to a future of greatness through unshakable faith. Our Father has been known for His faithfulness of providing peace, power, protection, and a plan for life's adversities. God said that He will give us unshakable faith, as we trust Him with our lives.

RENEWING THE MIND

What does the renewing of the mind mean? It means interpreting life through the lens of God's Word and the inspiration of the Holy Spirit. However, in my case through the lens of rejection, woundedness and or the opinions of others. Romans 12:2 (ISV) says, "Do not be conformed to this world, but continuously be transformed by the renewing of your minds so that you may be able to determine what God's will is—what is proper, pleasing, and perfect." This must be done with the knowledge of God's Word. It also requires a willingness and a desire to change. You must spend time with God as He is the One who renews our minds. My behavior begins in my mind, my mind is also my intellect, how I reason, and my intentions. My desire for spiritual transformation first happened within my mind. Everything starts in the mind. A thought starts in the mind as a personal belief.

I started the renewing of the mind by simply asking God to protect, to direct and to keep my mind firmly on Him. The Spirit waits for the believer to voluntarily surrender and abandon self, so that with the active cooperation of the believer's intellect may spread into the renewed mind. My journey to renewing my mind began with truth journaling. Truth journaling is your thoughts written down, usually of different problems such as worry, insecurity, working on goals and anything else that could have a negative condemnation. I read scriptures that spoke directly to the very thought and then I would truth journal the scripture for understanding and application. This was life changing for me. It allowed me to focus and gain a better understanding of the scripture. Truth journaling provided self-control, spiritual peace, and joy, which brought me ever so closer to God more than ever before.

As Christians, we are required to renew our minds, otherwise we will continue to walk in defeat, struggle, and confusion. Renewing your mind aligns your mind with the truth of God's Word, therefore, recognizing or realizing the lies of the enemy, and knowing and focusing on the truth of God's Word, His Word, is the replacement. I learned that renewing your mind is not just a spiritual process, it is physiological as well. When we decide to align with God's Word, this is the beginning of a new pathway in our brain to make that process preferable, which is the best practice in life. Our thoughts are the creation of life boundaries. If we want to experience a different life, the abundant life that God promised we must learn to be intentional with renewing our minds. We must master the process of renewing our mind in addition to recognizing the lies of the enemy.

Whenever we are faced with thoughts that do not align with God we must reject and replace it with thoughts that are agreeable with the plans that God has for our lives. We should also ask the Holy Spirit to bring to our remembrance a scripture that is opposite of the negative thoughts we encounter. Then you can truth journal and began to apply God's Word accordingly. Another great tool is to visualize. God created us with an amazing imagination and the ability to see, feel, sense and to be creative with innovative ideas and realities within our mind before they come into the physical realm. We must have both sight and vision. Over time the subconscious mind will become aware and convinced of the truth you are aligning your heart with, thus relinquishing the old and accepting the renewal of the mind.

Declaring scripture is another tool that I practice. I would highly recommend transforming scripture into a declaration. During my time of intimacy with God, I intentionally speak declarations over myself, and I do so with purpose. I meditate and visualize about the declarations that I speak. When we give God control, the presence of the Holy Spirit moves providing spiritual peace, and internal/ physical healing. It all comes down to the renewing of the mind.

Life is so impressive and when I look back and realize that we can come into all the riches of Christ by simply committing to renewing our minds. Renewing is beneficial to one's life. Remember to keep this as a thought, that the renewing of our minds will align our minds with the truth of God's Word. By the reading of scriptures, declaration, meditation, and applying God's Word to our lives, we can renew our minds on His Word, which will be most beneficial to us in our Christian walk.

SUFFICIENT GRACE

Ifeoma Esonwune

Certified Executive Coach, Speaker, and Trainer

ABOUT THE AUTHOR

Ifeoma Esonwune is a Certified Executive Coach, Speaker, and Trainer with over five years of experience and expertise in helping women discover their innate strength and abilities to perform and excel in their personal and professional lives. Hence, living a joy-filled, purposeful life with much success and great potential for significant accomplishments.

Having discovered her unique talents, purpose, and abilities, and utilized them to transform her life, she now helps other women do likewise. Ifeoma is a multi-award winner, leadership and business strategist, publisher, podcaster, communications strategist, DEI advocate, and a serial entrepreneur hired to speak and facilitate workshops and seminars at leading organizations, universities, and not-for-profits — nationally and internationally.

She offers individual and group coaching and mentoring, workshops, seminar facilitation and other training programs.

For speaking engagements, workshop/seminar facilitation, individual/group coaching, and team building:

- Email: ifeoma@starwomensnetwork.com OR

- https://www.johncmaxwellgroup.com/ifeomaesonwune/Contact

SUFFICIENT GRACE

"But he said to me, "My grace is sufficient for you, for my power is made perfect in weakness." Therefore I will boast all the more gladly about my weaknesses, so that Christ's power may rest on me. That is why, for Christ's sake, I delight in weaknesses, in insults, in hardships, in persecutions, in difficulties. For when I am weak, then I am strong." 2 Corinthians 12:9-10 (NIV)

"God is good; all the time" was how we greeted fellow brethren growing up in my local religious community in Enugu State, Nigeria. A phrase that I have grown to love and use in my daily life. An affirmation that God lives and sees me, and that His thoughts are always good towards me. Which is true-to-life; otherwise, I wouldn't be here, alive and thriving today.

In fact, on April 12, 2020, my faith was put to the test. I sent out Resurrection messages to family, colleagues, and friends about the gloriousness of Christ's resurrection. I sang "Alleluia. Christ is Risen" as I stirred the stew pot cooking on my stove.

It was Easter Sunday morning. I was happy and joyfully speaking with my sister-in-law, who was on the other end of the phone from Africa, but the continuous incoming call from my brother (also in Africa) wouldn't stop, so I put the first call on hold to take the incoming call from my brother.

"Papa just passed," my brother muttered with a shaky voice I hardly recognized. Those words pierced through my soul like a double-edged sword. The pain that engulfed me was so intense that my feet wobbled as my head spun around like I was in a three-ring circus. I couldn't articulate my thought. I guess I blanked out for a minute.

My heart was immediately heavy –with much grief and the pain overwhelmed me. For a minute, it felt like the gloriousness of Easter was a myth. Otherwise, how could a day so highly proclaimed suddenly turn into doom, gloom, and despair! Needless to say, my joy of Easter vanished abruptly.

My father, my confidant, my rock, had just passed?!? How can death visit someone so good on a day Christ conquered death? My whole world went dark and gloomy. And the only words I could say were, God, why? So, I cursed that Easter morning, and the subsequent Sundays weren't the same anymore.

Yes, grief overwhelmed me as I questioned God's goodness at that moment. My heart was saddened that it became a fertile ground for doubt and unbelief. My faith was shaken!

I had more questions than answers. And the enemy whispered all the thoughts my "miserable self" wanted to hear in that moment of agony. Words like *"Now, where's your risen Christ? Where's the joy of the resurrection? If this is God's goodness, of what use is it?"*

The devil saw an open window, and he rolled temptation in with might, which filled my heart with fear, anger and defeating thoughts, all of which felt good in my pain. Because, after all, where was God when everything Easter represented for me was taken away in a glimmer of light with a sad phone call?

I doubted God's goodness. How could He be good and let this happen? I had not seen my dad in more than five years. He had been in a serious accident, and he encountered several serious injuries. I had just spoken with him days before, and I was scheduled to talk to him later that afternoon. I also had plans to visit him, but with the COVID-19 pandemic, the lockdown restricted me.

The travel restrictions made matters worse. I couldn't be at the funeral nor pay my last respect in person. Depression took me over. I shut down, and I blamed myself: If only I had been with him, maybe I could have kept him alive – yes, I cursed that Easter Sunday.

Truthfully, temptations come to us to pressure and break

us. Challenging moments follow our moments of delight, making us question the actual existence of God.

I had prayed fervently for my dad's recovery. He suffered lots of trauma and pain from the accident, so of course, I had asked God to restore his health. He endured surgeries after surgeries, and I trusted God, but it seemed to me that He had, like, let me down when I needed Him the most. Yes, indeed, my faith wavered!

I tossed and turned most nights following my dad's passing, wondering why God didn't answer my prayers.

I was uncertain as to how these thoughts worked their way into my mind and overwhelmed me. Caging me in fear and anxiety, and ultimately, leaving me exhausted and wavering in my faith. I was drained in agony, tired, and frustrated with living.

But, when the Word of God is alive in your heart, it pushes you to choose God. Believe in Him and keep that faith rather than wallowing in doubt, agony, and grief.

It took a while, but I realized that God lives, and He still cares for me. The risen Christ is the same yesterday, today and forever. He is "The Good Shepherd."

I knew I had a choice to make. The pain I felt in my heart had led me to doubt my faith in God. But it was refreshing to hear that God had not forsaken me –that

He had not forgotten me. Recognizing what the devil was trying to do, I knew my best option was to cling to God no matter how unreal it seemed at the time.

Yes, He truly is the Good Shephard! He would leave the ninety-nine and search for the one lost sheep – that was me. Christ, the risen one, my risen Savior, is the giver of peace and joy.

If we seek Him...if we truly seek Him with our whole heart, we will find Him. If we open our hearts to Him, He showers us with love and restores purpose to our lives. He never leaves us as orphans.

God saw me through pain and misery. He held me up and put me on His shoulders. His Spirit manifested in me as I drew closer to Him through His Word and words of comfort. Even though I had gone astray, He saw my struggles, redirected my feet, and pulled me closer to Himself. And then, I knew I had nothing to fear. I understood that His plans for me were of good and not of evil.

"No temptation has overtaken you except what is common to mankind. And God is faithful; he will not let you be tempted beyond what you can bear. But when you are tempted, he will also provide a way out so that you can endure it." 1 Corinthians. 10:13 (NIV)

If you are facing difficulties or have lost a loved one, trust in God completely. Although we feel deserted sometimes, God is love. He is still with us and He cannot give us an overwhelming burden. In fact, when we feel overwhelmed, He carries us on His shoulders. Therefore, Christ calls us to take up our cross daily and follow Him.

So, my faith has remained unshakable in God. I know that "Yea, though I walk through the valley of the shadow of death, I will fear no evil; For You are with me; Your rod and Your staff, they comfort me." Psalm 23:4 (NKJV)

The psalmist reassures us that God is always with us, even in trials and temptations – God is always good.

"Blessed is the one who perseveres under trial because, having stood the test, that person will receive the crown of life that the Lord has promised to those who love him." James 1:12 (NIV)

FAITH THE SIZE OF A MUSTARD SEED

Sheila Farr

CEO of Gulf Coast Training
& Education Services, LLC
13x best-selling author, educator, and business strategist

ABOUT THE AUTHOR

Sheila Farr is an eternal optimist! She's the CEO of Gulf Coast Training & Education Services, LLC, in Biloxi, Mississippi, where she helps individuals and small businesses overcome obstacles and achieve their dreams by developing personalized business strategies that work.

Sheila is a multiple times international best-selling author and a cheerleader for others. She motivates people through her blog, "Thankful and Blessed 365," and is the founder of "Biloxi Reads!", which is a literacy initiative along the Mississippi Gulf Coast. Sheila also enjoys serving her community and the State of Mississippi as the Workforce Readiness Director for both the regional and state chapters of the Society for Human Resources Management.

Sheila loves to connect with people via her website: www.gulfcoasttraining.org or on social media sites such as Facebook, Instagram, and LinkedIn.

- Facebook: https://www.facebook.com/trainthegulfcoast
- IG: https://www.instagram.com/shefarr37/
- LinkedIn: https://www.linkedin.com/in/sheila-farr-20b35142/
- Blog site: https://thankfulandblessed365.com/

Faith the Size of a Mustard Seed

It's easy to trust God when things are going great in your life, but what happens when the challenging times come, and your faith gets tested? As Christians, we are called to display great faith and be encouraged in both the hills and the valleys of life. It's easy to say this when you're trying to encourage others or when things are going well for you, but do we really live this when hard times hit our own lives?

One of the most compelling verses in the Bible comes from Mark 4:32, (CSB) which says, "And when sown, it comes up and grows taller than all the garden plants, and produces large branches, so that the birds of the sky can nest in its shade." It's a verse about how the mustard seed (the smallest of all seeds), when planted, grows, and becomes the largest of all garden plants, and serves not only its original purpose, but also provides food and shelter for several other garden visitors. In this particular passage, Jesus was explaining how incredible Heaven is, as it provides for all, but I find this compelling because I also believe He was letting us know that if we have the tiniest bit of faith, He can turn that into blessings that not only meet our needs, but also allows us to meet the needs of others – or perhaps it is a reminder that if you have a bit of faith and you step out in obedience, He will not only calm your fear and uncertainty, but He will also provide an abundance of blessings to fill your life!

Not too long ago, I was in a situation at work where I had outgrown my position and was ready to make a change in my career. As a single career woman, I had a specific salary requirement to meet and maintain my monthly obligations, so walking away from a high-paying position with security and stepping into the unknown of entrepreneurship felt like a big gamble for me. I secured a part-time job so I could be sure my monthly obligations were met, so I made a plan in my business so I could experience steady growth; then I set my plan into action. Just a week before my transition, my part-time job opportunity disintegrated. I was left without that safety net for my finances, and I was terrified. At first, I panicked. Then I cried. Then I panicked again. I mean, how could this happen? I'd prayed, planned, and done all the things that a responsible business owner needed to do to be prepared for a transition. How could something that seemed so certain just vanish like that overnight? Well, as you know, when you're dealing with people, anything can happen, so I decided to take a few days and pray. Finally, I hit my knees and offered up my shaky situation to the Lord. I asked God for the faith to continue to move forward with my plan without having that safety net of a back-up salary. I prayed for Him to make a way for me, while continuing to walk toward my dream of being an entrepreneur without reliance on anyone but Him. I asked for BIG faith and a mindset of abundance!

As you might guess, when you open the door of your life and allow the Lord to walk in, miracles begin to happen! This is certainly true for my situation. I decided to make, specifically, praying for my business as part of my morning Prayer routine and within just a few hours (did you hear me say in just a few hours?) my phone and my Email began to fill up with requests for my services. I had friends who wanted to partner with me in collaboration for special projects. I had business owners needing my help with various aspects of their businesses. I had community leaders hiring me to consult with them on special projects. I had an abundance of work to do! What the devil had sent and meant to try to shake and break me, the Lord had turned my situation around and used it as a testimony to the importance of developing that mustard seed of faith! The Lord has, and He continues to bless me beyond belief! These days, I not only have a thriving business, but I am also able to help and nurture other budding businesses. I have a space to offer entrepreneurs and small businesses when they need a location to meet or train. I can and I do help my community by offering free services. I am positively impacting lives daily, simply because I hit my knees and displayed a mustard seed-sized faith!

Maybe you're reading this today and you're facing an uncertain situation. Maybe you feel discouraged or hopeless. Maybe your faith has been a bit shaken, and your mind is cluttered with fear and a "lack" mentality. If this is you today, let me offer you a bit of hope in that when you remind yourself that the Lord formed you to be a person of faith, hope, and love, those little negative things that disappoint, confuse, and steal the life from you can be recognized and released, allowing you to focus more fully on the blessings in your life instead of the blunders. When you offer your struggle to the Lord, He will cover you more fully and more completely than you could ever imagine! Today I am thankful for God's guiding hand on my life and for a spirit of fearlessness. You can't achieve extraordinary things if you have the weight of fear holding you back. God designed us to live joyful lives of abundance; not fearful lives of down-trodden worry. If you're facing something too big to handle alone, don't be afraid to hit your knees and ask for help. Plant that mustard seed of faith, and then step back and watch how the Lord will rain down blessings in your life.

LIVE BY FAITH

Rev. Suzette Hampton

A minister, realtor, entrepreneur, author, mother of four (4), and grandmother to eight (8) grandchildren. Founder of Trees of Righteousness Women's Ministry

ABOUT THE AUTHOR

Born and raised in the Washington Metropolitan area, Suzette Hampton is a minister, realtor, entrepreneur, author, mother of four (4), and grandmother to eight (8) grandchildren.

From an early age, she was taught the value and honor of serving others and she brings this core value to bear in every area of her life. She serves in various capacities with hard work, integrity, and dedication.

She is founder of Trees of Righteousness Women's Ministry where she encourages, empowers, and strengthens women to reach their full potential in God by providing opportunities for spiritual growth and development, meaningful fellowship, and a welcoming, safe, and supportive environment in which to confront and be healed from spiritual, mental, and emotional pain and trauma. She is actively involved in her community and is particularly passionate about assisting the homeless in her area.

Live by Faith

> *"For whatever is born of God overcomes the world. And this is the victory that has overcome the world—our faith."*
> *1 John 5:4*

When I was young, I believed my life would be perfect. I planned to graduate from high school at the top of my class, attend college with an academic scholarship, and double-major in journalism and business management. I dreamed of writing important, life-changing stories that would cause people's hearts to smile and that I would write books that would always have happy endings. I envisioned owning my own companies, making lots of money, and living a very easy life with access to all the bells and whistles. What I didn't understand back then was that life isn't perfect and it doesn't always work out the way we'd like.

I was eight months pregnant when I graduated from high school. Although I finished near the top of my class, I didn't have any academic scholarships. I flunked out of my first semester at the junior college in my area because I didn't have the tools necessary to be a new, first-time mom AND a college freshman taking classes on TV. I never had the opportunity to live a life of luxury. But I have had the privilege of living a life of faith.

I learned early on that constant attention to the Word of God, and time spent reading, hearing, and studying it, produces faith. Romans 10:17 states, "So then faith comes by hearing, and hearing by the word of God." From my youth, I heard the Word of God preached by Pastors at church on Sundays and taught by ministers at Bible studies on Wednesdays. I heard the Word taught to my family by my father on Fridays and in the words of songs sung by choirs. I read it aloud to my siblings and recited verses I had memorized. My faith in God was established by hearing the Word and it has been the foundation on which my life has been built.

I'll be completely honest and admit that living a life of faith has not always been easy. In fact, it's been full of surprises, challenges, unexpected occurrences, unplanned events, and situations beyond my control. Many of the challenges I faced were results of my poor choices and decisions. Some of the most trying times in my life were those times when I believed I deserved what I was going through because I had messed up. Through it all, though, I held on to my faith. During physical and emotional abuse, eviction, and divorce, my faith endured. With resentment, anger, and unforgiveness swirling around inside me, I chose to hold on to my faith. When faced with some of the most difficult decisions I've ever made, my faith pointed me in the direction of the Creator of all things, my Sovereign, loving and faithful God.

"Now faith is the substance of things hoped for, the evidence of things not seen."Hebrews 11:1

One might wonder how I could have faith in what (or Who) I could not see.

I had faith because God IS! He is Yahweh, the Self-Existing One. He is El Shaddai, the All-Sufficient God! He is the Everlasting God – the same yesterday, today, and forever! He is my King – my Lord, Savior, and Redeemer! I had faith because God is my Source, my Provider, my Defense, and my Strong Tower! He is the God Who raised His Son, Jesus, from the dead and sent us a Helper in the form of the Holy Spirit! He is the Author and Finisher of my faith!

I continue to have faith because I KNOW the Lord for myself. I am in relationship with Him. I have faith because I've communed with Him in worship and cried out to Him in prayer. I've sat quietly and listened for the sound of His still small voice. I have faith because He has proven Himself to me over and over again. I have exchanged my heaviness and burdens for His peace and rest, and He has ALWAYS kept His promises to me. I have faith because He has healed and delivered me and freed me from the lies of the enemy. I trust Him fully and completely and I know that wherever I go, in whatever condition I find myself, He is with me.

Acknowledging these truths has helped to redirect my focus from my challenges back to God. Each time I do that, I experience total peace – peace that only He can provide. I have come to understand that I am NOT the sum of my mistakes, my past, and my emotions. Instead, I am a work in progress. I consistently strive to redefine myself to ensure that I don't (and won't) settle for less than what I deserve from myself and for myself. I have realized that my relationship with the Lord is not based on what I do right, how well I perform, or how perfect I try to be. My relationship with Him is based on His unconditional love for me and my willingness to receive it.

My life hasn't worked out the way I had planned and I'm totally fine with that. Knowing that God created me with great purpose and that His will for my life is perfect trumps any plans I had or could ever have for myself. He is in control and my life is in His hands. Romans 1:17 says "For in it the righteousness of God is revealed from faith to faith; as it is written, "The just shall live by faith." I choose to live by faith in the God Who knew me before I was formed in my mother's womb, (see Psalm 139:13). I choose to live by faith in the God Who filled me with the gifts, skills, talents, and abilities I've been given to pour out into and upon the earth. I choose to live by the faith that has been cultivated through what I've heard, seen, and experienced. I choose to live by faith.

QUESTIONS TO PONDER

1. Is your faith strong enough to trust God through tests and trials?

2. Are you willing to surrender your plans for your life in favor of God's plans?

3. Can your faith be used to positively affect change in others?

MY CONVERSATION WITH GOD

Dr. Essie M. McKoy

Award-Winning Educator
7x's Amazon Best-Selling Author and International Best-Selling Author
Host of #1 Podcast Dr. Essie Speaks Education
President/CEO of Dr. Essie Speaks Educational Consulting, LLC

ABOUT THE AUTHOR

Dr. Essie McKoy, an award-winning educator, #1 podcast host, and a 7x's Amazon and International best-selling author, received her Doctorate in Education (Ed.D.) and an Educational Specialist Degree (Ed. S.) from the University of North Carolina at Greensboro, a master's degree from Appalachian State University, and a Bachelor of Science Degree from Winston-Salem State University. She has many areas of certification in NC and VA and attended a multitude of leadership programs throughout the nation.

She is the President and CEO of her own Educational Consulting Business, Dr. Essie Speaks. Dr. McKoy is a Lead Education Writer and serves in an area of her expertise in a local school district within the District of Columbia, Maryland, and Virginia (DMV). Furthermore, you will hear the gifted and talented Dr. McKoy, on her weekly #1 podcast, Dr. Essie Speaks Education.

Dr. McKoy has received many awards and accolades for her service in the field of education. Feel free to visit her website at www.dressiespeaks.com.

MY CONVERSATION WITH GOD

"Now faith is the [a]substance of things hoped for, the [b]evidence of things not seen." – Hebrews 11:1

Dear God,

I cannot see You. I cannot hear You. There are days I cannot even feel You. I cannot see Your presence in the world. I cannot hear Your voice. I cannot see Your presence in my life. There is so much destruction, so much sadness, so much hate, so much malice, and so much of pure wickedness. I feel like the weight of the world is on my shoulders. God, where are You?

There are days I long for You. I call Your name and it seems like I am not even Your child. I have heartaches, pains, and tears of sadness. I do not know which way to go, where to turn, or what steps to take. I kneel, I pray, I meditate, I ponder, and I look to you for help. Walls are crashing down all around me. God, where are you?

Father, why do you let me experience the loneliness, the dark days, and dreary nights; days of anxiety, depression, and even suicide; days of regret, days of tension and stress, days of having no one to turn to and nowhere to go. I am emotionally bankrupt, financially strained, and spiritually empty! I have many insecurities and I constantly deal with low self-esteem. I have no place to stay, no clothes to wear, and no food to eat. I have no vision for tomorrow. I have been both abused and misused and I've encountered failure after failure. I am in despair and in need of you. God, where are you?

I ask for your guidance, as my Heavenly Father, my Lord, my Savior. I ask for Your grace and Your mercy over my life. I ask for Your deliverance of my soul. I ask for Your protection. I ask for Your forgiveness. I ask for Your spirit to permeate my being. I ask for Your goodness to follow me. I ask for Your love to penetrate my heart. I ask for Your helping hand. I need to hear Your voice. I need to see Your face. I need you to set me free. Free my mind and free my spirit. Help me to love myself so I can respect myself. Give me Your glory. Shower me with Your peace and fill me with Your happiness. Stomp out what is evil within me. I need Your touch. I need Your spirit to enter my space. I need Your majestical power of healing. I need Your presence. I need a miracle. I need you! God, where are you?

You are The Almighty, omnipotent, the way maker, the Father of healing, the Father of life, the Father of peace and happiness, and the Father of Agape love. You can make my crooked path straight. You can make my long nights short. You can make my midnight tears turn into laughter. You can make my hurt turn into healing. You can take what was meant for evil and turn it into good. You can take my pain and turn it into my purpose. You can make my dreams manifest. You can give me glory and allow me to uplift Your name. You can give me an ear to hear. You can let me whisper Your name. God, I feel Your presence!

I need to have the faith to believe that whatever I ask in Your name, it shall be granted. I need to have the faith that Your love is sufficient. I need to have the faith that you can make the impossible possible. I need to have the faith I will be blessed, and my children will be blessed. I need to have the faith that you know what is good for my life. I need to have the faith that I can do all things through you who gives me strength. I need to have the faith that my problems will have solutions. I need to have the faith that my brokenness will help to develop my wholeness. I need to have the faith that You will be there when no one else is. God, I feel Your presence!

Cast Your spirit of faith upon my soul! Cast Your joy within me. Cast Your light on me. Cast Your divine presence around me. Cast Your love through me. Cast Your blessings over me. God, I feel Your presence.

I have faith in You! I trust You! I am assured and have confidence in Your ability to do Your works in me. I declare to live a faithful life. I give You, my service. I render my life to You. I will obey Your call on my life.

Your presence in my life comforts me. I believe in You. I hope for things that I have not seen and know that it shall come to pass. God, I feel Your presence.

I believe in Your healing powers. I believe that You can heal the sick. I believe that You can make the blind to see. I believe You can make the deaf hear. I believe that You can make the lame walk. I believe in Your Son, Jesus. God, I feel Your presence in my life.

You delivered me. You saved me. You gave me another chance at life. You freed me from my addictions. You healed me from my hurt. You came to my rescue. You gave me a new life. You restored my soul. You gave me hope. You redeemed me. You took me as I was and made me whole. You gave me life and gave it more abundantly. You gave me the ability to call Your name. You gave me the desires of my heart. You gave me my existence. You gave me everything. God, I feel Your presence and now I walk by FAITH!

A Time for Reflection

1. God, where are You? Have you ever felt like God was not present in your life? Reflect upon that moment.

2. God, I feel Your presence. How did you develop strong faith? Reflect upon that moment.

3. Write your prayer to God!

TRAUMA VALIDATED IN CHRIST

Syreeta Moody

CEO of Special Hands Outreach
Professional School Counselor
An advocate of mental and emotional health

ABOUT THE AUTHOR

Syreeta Moody is the CEO of Special Hands Outreach, LLC and a Professional School Counselor who has been in the education system for 15 years.

Syreeta's passion is helping disproportionate children achieve academic success, develop an understanding of college/career opportunities, and foster the development of effective social skills and emotional regulation when faced with difficult circumstances.

Her time in the education system has revealed many areas of common everyday needs, as well as special needs, with the largest area being in the trauma and adverse childhood experiences which can affect children's brain development and hinders academic growth and daily life fulfillment. As an advocate to their mental and emotional health, Syreeta's charge is to be the change agent that takes the time to walk alongside a child to find freedom from their trauma experiences and to help develop their strengths to inspire and empower change so that they are free to be their best selves.

TRAUMA VALIDATED IN CHRIST

"And the Lord said to Satan, "Behold, all that he has is in your power; only do not lay a hand on his person.". Job 1:12

Trauma that is validated in Christ means that God has allowed the experience of deeply distressing and disturbing situations that challenge the ability to manage and regulate mental thoughts, emotional responses, and limit social functions in one's daily life. Why would a loving God allow something like this to happen? Many unbelievers, and believers alike, have often asked this question. We often think of suffering as a bad thing and many times we come out looking at the experience from a wounded mindset instead of a warrior mindset. Instead of saying "I'm so damaged from this experience" you might say "Look how much I've grown from this experience." You survived something you had no idea you were capable of doing. Our thoughts and the way we see things really drive who and how we approach the journey of life. If we are to follow the template of Jesus Christ who was born in the same flesh that we have been born in, we should not be surprised that we will, as believers, walk in His proverbial shoes in this life and experience various trials and tests just as Jesus experienced. In fact, in James 1:2-4 it says "My brethren, count it all joy when you fall into various trials, knowing that the testing of your faith produces patience. But let patience have its perfect work, that you may be perfect and complete, lacking nothing." Jesus left us a blueprint for how to conquer life's trials and how to grow from those trials in His Word. However, this is a revelation I now know to be a result of the trauma I've experienced. Getting through it seemed slow and never ending, but each step was a necessary process for the road ahead that God had for me.

The road I was on needed to be redirected and this had to happen fast. I needed my focus off of me and back on God. When I came to myself, like the prodigal son, I looked around and I had to face the faulty decisions I had made that left me single with six children and four failed toxic relationships. I'm the daughter of a Pastor and I did not want to be obedient to God at the time; I wanted to do things my way and on my own. I was rebellious and stubborn. This is exactly what God allowed me to do and it came at a high cost of my self-esteem, confidence, disappointment with myself, freedom, missed opportunities, and no hope for dating or marriage. I felt so alone, I was lonely, and I was often depressed. My will for my life needed to be redirected to God's will for my life, and while I thought I knew what I wanted for myself, I needed to seek God desperately to find out what He wanted for me, from me, and through me. See Proverbs

16:9 "A man's heart plans his way, But the Lord directs his steps." I know that God supports us in making plans for our lives, however it is with His direction that we must take the appropriate steps. Although I do believe my plans were in God's will, that I would go to college, obtain my dream job, get married, have kids, and serve God's people with my family, but, nonetheless, I took a few wrong turns and made decisions that pulled me further and further away from the protective covering of God. I finally had enough of the struggle, the hurt, and sadness in my heart. I had to come to a screeching halt, pour my heart out to God and surrender completely. I had to deny myself of the things I wanted that were outside of His will, and that was so difficult, and also, I had to truly commit to everything that came along with following Christ. See Matthew 16:24, "Then Jesus said to His disciples, "If anyone desires to come after Me, let him deny himself, and take up his cross, and follow Me."

I had to make a change to see different outcomes. Changing involved me redefining my decision-making process and wholeheartedly trusting God. Trusting where and what He was leading me to. Although I had no clue what was next, I now felt comforted, and I had confidence that I was not alone. See Deuteronomy 31:6-8, "Be strong and of good courage, do not fear nor be afraid of them; for the Lord your God, He is the One who goes with you. He will not leave you nor forsake you. Then

Moses called Joshua and said to him in the sight of all Israel, "Be strong and of good courage, for you must go with these people to the land which the Lord has sworn to their fathers to give them, and you shall cause them to inherit it. And the Lord, He is the One who goes before you. He will be with you, He will not leave you nor forsake you; do not fear nor be dismayed." God affirmed me in a way that gave me peace that passed even my understanding as well as everyone else's understanding. People would ask me, "How are you doing it, raising six kids on your own and you still have your sanity?" During each and every situation, circumstance, life issues and challenges -even if it didn't make sense, if I didn't want to do it, and if I had to do it alone, I trusted God. I called upon Him for everything. At first it was very uncomfortable, but when I called on Him, He answered me, and this was how God increased my faith in Him. God did what He said He would do. I started to see a pattern with God when my decisions were aligned with His counsel and the Holy Spirit would make sure that my path would remain straight. See, Proverbs 3:5-6, "Trust in the Lord with all your heart, And lean not on your own understanding; In all your ways acknowledge Him, And He shall direct your paths."

So, when I got back on the path of righteousness with my decisions and started trusting God, many outcomes have changed, and I now walk with a renewed mind, renewed spirit, and a renewed faith. See, Romans 12:2, And do not be conformed to this world, but be transformed by the renewing of your mind, that you may prove what is that good and acceptable and perfect will of God."

Trauma validated in Christ means that God has allowed these life experiences (deeply distressing and disturbing situations) –to show me that living life my own way, where the regulating of thoughts and emotions were concerned, that it is next to impossible without God. God wanted me to understand that with Him my mental thoughts, emotional responses, and social interactions are all filtered through the Holy Spirit operating in connection with my faith. It is now clear to me, more than ever, that traumatic situations are going to come in and out of my life until I draw my last breath, but renewing my mind daily, staying in the Word of God, and keeping my mind fixed on God will give me that perfect peace in my situation –in any situation. See, Isaiah 26:3 "You will keep him in perfect peace, Whose mind is stayed on You, Because he trusts in You." When I fix my mind, heart, and spirit on God and His Word, I am secure in God's amazing love and infinite power.

QUESTIONS TO PONDER

1. What traumatic experiences have you faced?

2. What areas in your life do you need to redirect?

3. What steps will you take to get to a renewed life in Christ?

HOW TO HANDLE THE CHALLENGES OF LIFE

Shirley Murphy

Nigerian Journalist, Author
Publisher of Global Labour Events
and Business Magazine (GLEBM)

ABOUT THE AUTHOR

Shirley Murphy is a Nigerian Journalist based in Abuja, Nigeria's federal capital city. She is currently the Publisher of Global Labour Events and Business Magazine (GLEBM), an online independent specialized publication; she is a TV show host and a media consultant, as well as an international speaker. She has authored three books, "The Ideal Parents", "5 Steps to Purpose Actualization" and "The Power of Praise".

She is the brain behind two Non-Governmental Organizations (NGOs), Proud Parents International and Women Reach Out with God Initiative (WROWGI). She believes in collaborating and supporting the advancement of women across the world. Shirley is a life and family therapist, who has transformed the lives of many, especially women and girls in Nigeria. She is very passionate about women's education and empowered to ensure that women all over the world become more visible and in control of their lives. She is extremely compassionate and passionate in giving hope to many women in her sphere of influence.

She is blessed to have both a loving husband and devoted children.

Visit her online at https://www.facebook.com/profile.php?id=100009479577778

HOW TO HANDLE THE CHALLENGES OF LIFE

"And not only that, but we also glory in tribulations, knowing that tribulation produces perseverance; and perseverance, character; and character, hope. Now hope does not disappoint, because the love of God has been poured out in our hearts by the Holy Spirit who was given to us." Romans 5:3-5

The life we have and live comes with many challenges, and we know that challenges of life never come to break you, but to make, build, strengthen, redirect, redefine and renew you. But in all of it, you must be ready to accept it when it comes; we must be prepared to learn and intentionally grow in the process. We often complain with words or questions like, Why me? Why not you! In everything God has admonished us to always give thanks to Him, because He said, He will never give us more than we can handle, meaning that the challenges you may be going through right now, you can handle it/them. If only you can stoop down to see God in the moment! If only you will focus on the manual (the Word of God) for solutions. If only, you'll trust Him in the process. If only your faith can be as little as that of the mustard seed. He said, He will never leave you nor forsake you. So many times, we often see everything that comes our way as negative. We have unfortunate thoughts like, God does not love me!! You blaspheme with your mouth instead of rejoicing for He had conquered the battle or our challenges so that we could have a better life in Him. When you are negative about everything around you, it will be impossible to see anything good. There's no one, living nor anyone who has passed on, who has succeeded in life without challenges; know that your mindset in the time of challenges will determine if you'll conquer or be defeated. The decision is with you, so you decide if you want to come out victorious or damaged.

REDIRECT

Redirecting your thoughts, your mind, your expectations, and belief to the God of the process is a very effective way to handling whatever challenges that may come your way. So many times, we allow our inner voice of negativity to bind us and make us feel defeated. That voice, when you allow it to run rampant, will make you believe that God is not able to turn things around in your challenges. You see, those are the same old tricks of the devil, so you must be wise not to allow him to steal your joy and make you remain in the valley.

So many people have allowed seeds of negativity to be sown into them and this negativity has grown so much in them that all they see are negative situations with negative outcomes. Well, I'm not interested in knowing just how much you have allowed the devil to cheat you and steal your joy, but what I want to tell you is that in this chapter you will learn that you have a responsibility to shut that voice up and begin to put on the "I can do all things through Christ" spirit and once you change your mindset and your confessions, you will then see yourself as an over comer with a victorious mindset; leave that defeated mindset behind!

Stop rehearsing all your mistakes and thinking about what you cannot do or how you do not have what it takes. It does not really matter how many times you fail, but what does matter is that God's Spirit will enable you to rise again. Learn from those unfortunate events; build up positive experiences and a positive mindset to winning big. Remind yourself: I am the child of the Most-High God, I can do all things through Christ (See Phil. 4:13, "I can do all things through Christ who strengthens me.") I have a bright future, I am talented; my story is different, I am favored, I will fulfil my purpose and destiny. I have what it takes to be different, and influential, I can make positive impacts in my generation. God loves me. No difficulty can put me down and my faith looks up to God.

Our daily internal dialogue must be positive and hopeful. You may have suffered a great loss; you may have had an unfair experience or people trying to pull you down. Your beginning may not have been pleasant, but don't allow that to pull or weigh you down into negativity. Redirect your faith unto the God who is able to make everything beautiful in His time, trust Him completely and always.

REDEFINE

Be redefined by the prophecies of God for your life and hold on to what He says concerning you, and your challenges will fade away. If you stay focused on the negative, you'll have a war on the inside. You cannot have a critical attitude towards yourself and expect God's best for you. Quit focusing on the wrongs you've done. God has already rolled away your shame, your past, your failures. It is up to you to do your part. Let it go so you can go into your Promised Land. Our faith is made effective when we acknowledge the good things that are in us. You don't apply faith in the negatives, the weaknesses, or past issues, but you do apply faith in hopeful situations. Redefine your life with affirmative words and do this daily.

On the positive side, I have talent, I will succeed, I have the favor of God, and I am blessed. This affirmation drives faith to benefit you. When we believe we have what it takes, we focus on the possibilities of achieving our best. Tell yourself, each day "I am actualizing my purpose." You are not just a housewife, common teacher, or just a businessman or woman. You are the child of the Most-High God. You have a purpose on earth, and you are fulfilling your destiny. So much has been deposited in you. You are not just anything, but a product of God's glory awaiting manifestation. Knowing and acknowledging these things can boost your confidence and help you become who God has created you to be faster than you can ever imagine.

RENEWED

Be transformed by the renewing of your mind. Then you will be able to test and approve what God's will is, His good, pleasing, and perfect will. See Romans 12:2 "Do not conform to the pattern of this world but be transformed by the renewing of your mind. Then you will be able to test and approve what God's will is—his good, pleasing and perfect will." (NIV)

No matter what you may be going through, staying positive, even in the face of challenges, is the one and only factor that will bring you out speedily and lead to your success. Stay focus, look onto God, have a renewed and changed mindset, believing that all things are possible with Christ.

Successful people usually look for the good in every

situation. No matter how many reversals and setbacks they experience, they expect to get something good out of everything that happens to them; they believe every setback is part of a great plan that is moving them towards achieving the outstanding success that is inevitable for them. Know that every situation that comes your way is to teach you and not to break you. Swing your thinking to the positive, and confess out loud, that no matter what happens, my peace, my faith is in God, and nothing can take that away or have it shaken. See Psalm 112:6-7, "Surely the righteous will never be shaken; they will be remembered forever. They will have no fear of bad news; their hearts are steadfast, trusting in the Lord."

God did not create any of us to be average. He didn't make us to just live –we were created to excel. The Bible says that God, from the beginning of the world knew us and chose us unto Himself and to His glory. He has equipped us with everything we need to live an abundant life, which means that you have seeds of greatness embedded on the inside of you, but it is up to you to believe and act on them.

Seeds are words. Words are seeds, and words have the creative power to reproduce. Therefore, make positive declarations over your life and things around you will begin to work for your good. As those positive and faith-fill words daily permeate your mind and especially your subconscious mind, it eventually will change the way you see yourself and change your beliefs. This will truly help renew you from the inside out.

FAITH IN GOD

Ruth Thomas-Oshun

A programs manager, a social science researcher, an advocate of women's self-empowerment, a motivational columnist, a speaker, and a community multicultural award winner, 2021.

ABOUT THE AUTHOR

Ruth Thomas-Oshun is a programs manager, a social science researcher, an advocate of women's self-empowerment, a motivational columnist, a speaker, and a community multicultural award winner, 2021.

Ruth's educational background is in Education and Social Work. She has several years of experience working with women and children, inspiring and motivating them to be self-determined and self-motivated about their own lives. She is committed to the principles of social justice and strives to grow and further her knowledge of emotional intelligence, the world, and other cultures around her.

Ruth's strong suites of skills include strong enthusiasm, empathy, perseverance, attentive listening skills, coaching, inspiring and motivating. She is an excellent supporter and collaborator in any working environment and partnership. Anywhere Ruth finds herself, she is bold to share that she is a believer of the Gospel of Jesus Christ.

She is a wife and a mother of three beautiful and wonderful children.

FAITH IN GOD

"But without faith it is impossible to please him: for he that cometh to God must believe that he is, and that he is a rewarder of them that diligently seek him."
Hebrews 11:6 KJV

Faith is the bedrock of walking with God. It is an absolute trust in God's integrity over all the affairs of our lives. It is based on the simplicity of the Gospel. It is about understanding God's system on the earth. In these interesting times, as believers, praying in faith is key to taking delivery of the more abundant life God has promised believers. To live by faith, we must guard the battle ground –our minds. The Word of God admonishes us to guard our heart with all diligence because out of it are the issues of life. See Proverbs 4:23 (KJV) As Paul said, "For though we walk in the flesh, we do not war after the flesh:" 2 Corinthians 10:3, KJV.

On my Christian journey, I have observed that whenever I am faced with any situation, I meditate on the scriptures relating to that situation. I would meditate on the Word of God concerning that situation, and I would start to say it out aloud, repeatedly and confess it, and once I break through in the spirit and I pray about it having no doubts in my heart, those words would make practical fulfilment in my life. The challenge is guarding my heart and declaring my faith based on the promises of God in the scriptures of the Bible. Any time I remember that God's thoughts for me are not of evil but of good, to give me prosperity materially, keep me in good health and prosperity spiritually (see Jeremiah 29:11), I get excited, and I focus my gaze on the Lord. I have been in some precarious situations where I've come to my wits' end, and sometimes, I start to think along the what if lines. Sometimes when I look at the facts, my mind struggles with muttering out and declaring God's promises toward that situation. However, He knows our frame, and so, while meditating on His words, my faith starts to develop in God. I would count all what God has done for me in the past and I would ask for His mercy and grace to confront the present challenges I might face. I would ask for the help of the Holy Spirit, bearing in mind that Jesus had settled it all for me when He died for all of mankind, and as a result of His death, burial and resurrection, I'm not supposed to be carrying the burden, but rather, He asked that I put all, not some, but all of my burdens upon Him for He cares for me (see, 1 Peter 5:7, NKJV). Standing on these promises, I start to make scriptural declarations based on the situation in faith and I give thanks for the answered prayers. Sometimes it amazes me how everything just turns out or around for my good.

I know that without faith it is impossible to please God.

So, I have an understanding that in this partnership, faith is very essential –the key requirement in pleasing God. I also know that my faith in God will often be tested (see James 1:2-4). His Word says our light affliction is but for a moment. So, I know that He rewards those that diligently seek Him (Hebrews 11:6). Another scripture I meditate upon regularly is that, if we as human beings that err, know how to give good gifts unto our children, how much more shall our Father which is in Heaven give good things to them that ask Him? See Luke 11:13. I find myself assured in Him when I think about this. For me, that means God is interested in my welfare, and He has made provisions for me, and not only that, He also loves me beyond my imagination. Therefore, as a child of God in this dispensation of grace, I am connected to the Source, who is Jesus, I also know that the scriptures cannot be broken; if God said it – then it is settled, because He is not a man that can go back on His Word. Life is beautiful, it's blissful and we must live in the abundance God said we could have (see John 10:10, KJV) for this is the heritage Christ has offered us by paying for all our debts, physically, emotionally, spiritually in every way on the cross. So, why would I not fully accept and leverage all that Christ's blood has already procured for me? It is imperative that as a lifestyle, we must rely on His promises for us and apply the Word of God in every area of our lives. It does not cost us anything, except to believe in Him.

The kind of faith Abraham had, that he staggered not at the promises of God is needed if we are going to operate in kingdom blessings. Yes, trying times come and they will continue to come, but if we are resolve that we will put all our trust in God, He would direct our paths and we would come out on the other side better off and worthy of His mercy and we will have and experience His peace that cannot be explained. After all, the plan of God for us is to live life more abundantly. Our responsibility is to serve God, worship Him and do His will and His will is for His children to have unshakable faith in Him. We may not know what the next moment will bring but we can rest assured that God will lead us, and we can trust Him all the way. This is the confidence that we have in Christ that when we ask anything from God through Christ, we will receive it. My prayer is that as we put all our trust in God, that we will receive His grace to lead triumphant and victorious lives because everything we need and will ever need is in Him.

May God bless *You* richly,

THE POWER IS WITHIN YOU

Dr. Daphne Soares

Founder and CEO of Carousel Moms Business and Leadership Coaching
A Business, Leadership, NLP Master Coach

ABOUT THE AUTHOR

Dr. Daphne Soares is the Founder and CEO of Carousel Moms Business and Leadership Coaching. She has been ranked #7 among the Top 30 Business Coaches for 2022 by The NYC Journal, Top Women Leaders in 2022 by Passion Vista and Top 10 Female Coaches in 2021 by Yahoo Finance. She is Amazon's #1 Best-selling author of "Don't Judge a Book by Its Cover", "Business Success", "Secrets to Business Success: How to start and run an online business in these challenging times", "Embracing Imperfections 2", and "Created for Greatness" with Les Brown, just to name a few.

Dr. Daphne is a certified Business, Leadership, NLP Coach and Timeline Therapist, author, international speaker, and mentor. She has gone from a 9-5 job to Homemaker, Confirmation Coordinator, Masters' Catechist, Counsellor, Hypnotherapist, and Psychotherapist. She is passionate about empowering women globally to find the right balance in their carousels of life, to create a thriving business, overcome limiting beliefs and set healthy boundaries. She conducts one-on-one and group-coaching, both online and offline.

Website: https://linktr.ee/carouselmoms

The Power is Within You

"Do not give up on your dreams. God has not given up on you. The best of you is yet within you, unleash your power and talent from within."

— Dr. Daphne Soares

I was born into a beautiful close-knit family of four in a small city, and I was the third child of my parents. My second sibling passed away soon after birth which broke my parents' hearts. They were very excited when I came along. As we grew up, our family increased with our partners coming along. My brother first got married and myself three years later.

Unplanned, my husband quickly received a job in the Gulf after we married, and we decided to take the opportunity. He had to leave immediately so we both decided I would return to stay with my parents until we could arrange for me to come to the Gulf. During that time, I was expecting our first baby; I left my senior executive 9-5 job as the birth of our baby drew near. I received a lot of pampering from my parents. When our baby was eight months old, I had to leave my parents and the country to join my husband: a new mom, a new place, and a new lifestyle.

Keeping our cultural and family values, I became a stay-at-home mom to personally raise our firstborn –our little princess. My husband would work long hours, and I had to learn to manage with no extended help. After a year, I became pregnant again and was expecting our second child. We were blessed with a bouncing baby boy. My husband had applied for annual leave which got rejected so I was blessed that my mom was able to come join us and assist me. Nine days before our sons' birth we got the shocking news that she lost her mother, my grandmother. My mother was torn between grief and joy.

When my mom flew back home, our two babies were the only human beings I would interact with. There were times when I needed my husband to talk to and help around the house and with the children. Internally, I felt so alone. As days went by, I started getting more and more burnt out.

When the kids started school things changed. I would use those hours to grab some sleep, clean, and cook so that when they returned home, I could teach, play, and spend quality time with them. We also registered them for weekly faith classes in our church. I would accompany them to church and wait around until they were finished, and my husband would come to pick us up. It gave me the opportunity to meet other parents. One day I heard an announcement that they needed faith teachers, and local training was starting soon. The timing was incredible, as it was during both the kids' catechism classes. I took advantage of this opportunity. By the grace of God, I completed my training and was assigned a class. My hard work and dedication led me to teach higher grades and I was quickly appointed as the coordinator for the Sacrament classes. I was also asked to be a lector and volunteer too. This sparked ideas of getting the kids to join the altar servers, the choir, and other ministries.

As the kids grew, expenses grew. I decided to start work, but I had no local work experience and my husband wanted me to remain a stay-at-home mom. I finally managed to help him understand the need that I go start work, so I started searching for employment. Schools would not hire me without the required teaching certifications. Once, I got an opportunity as an O Levels' Bible Study teacher since I had completed my master's certification in the faith from the United States. Someone I knew very well secretly applied for the position, and with a referral they got the job. This hurt me. I prayed and believed God had a greater plan for me.

As time went by, I stumbled on an online Psychology course and decided to give it a go. I could feel that mind shift, positive energies, and hunger for more knowledge in this direction. I went on to discover a Counselling Diploma and dug even deeper. This helped me to overcome stress, anxiety, fears, embrace challenging situations, stay happy, and maintain a positive mindset. I became more understanding of people and life situations. I loved it. I wasn't going to let go of this.

This was the starting point of my life-changing journey. I started asking myself what my purpose was in life? What legacy did I want to leave? I moved on and began creating an image of my ultimate self. I wrote everything down. I also discovered hidden talents within myself. I explored the different opportunities, so I decided to make a transition into coaching and invested my time into studying to be a Business, Leadership and NLP Coach.

Being a woman does not mean that we are destined only for giving birth, cleaning, cooking, raising the kids, and teaching them. We are worthy of so much more. Today, I stand confidently as a Business, Leadership, NLP, and Time-Line Therapy Coach. I am the Founder and CEO of my own business Carousel Moms Business and Leadership Coaching, which was the name created by our beautiful daughter. She explains, "a mom has many roles, and it is vital that mom has the right balance in her carousel of life and syncs to the right rhythm of the music." Our son, too, helps in different ways. I am proud of where I am today. I am a successful mompreneur (mom entrepreneur) and an inspiration to my children. I now serve internationally—as coach, counselor, NLP Master Coach, author, speaker, and mentor. I have been recognized and awarded globally several times by many countries. What is more beautiful is that I can live life on my own terms. I can now spend quality time with my kids and give them the attention and the love they need, I am the voice crying in the wilderness for women, and I am passionate about Empowering Women globally for success. Everything that we need is within us –if only we believe and trust in God and in ourselves.

QUESTIONS TO PONDER

1. What legacy do you want to leave for your family? Why?

2. In what ways do you inspire your kids and others around you?

3. What is stopping you from living your dreams, using your talents to the fullest and how can you change this?

FAITH MOVED MY MOUNTAINS

Vanessa Spence

An author, speaker, training consultant, and budget coach. An active member of Delta Sigma Theta Sorority, Inc., and the NETwork BICP.

ABOUT THE AUTHOR

Vanessa Spence is the mother of two daughters Michaela and Jordan, who have always been her motivation to do the work, break generational curses, and heal. Vanessa was born and raised in Raleigh, North Carolina, and graduated from North Carolina State University.

Vanessa is an author, speaker, budget coach, and training consultant with over 20 years of experience in the corporate sector. Vanessa is certified in both Crown Financial Ministry and Dave Ramsey's Financial Peace University, where she works with people in the community to build and grow wealth.

As an active volunteer in the community, Vanessa is a proud member of Delta Sigma Theta Sorority, Inc., a public service organization committed to sisterhood, scholarship, and service. She is also the VP of Professional Development and Talent for the NETwork BICP, whose mission is to continue transforming our future by empowering our members and our community.

FAITH MOVED MY MOUNTAINS

"For as the body without the spirit is dead, so faith without works is dead also." – James 2:26

My family and I were grieving the loss of my eldest brother, Larry, who passed on December 29, 2014. His death was an unexpected loss, and very difficult for my family to cope with.

Twenty-eight months later, I woke one morning, wondering if it was all just a bad dream, although, in my heart, I knew it was not. I still had my clothes on from the night before. My head hurt. My eyes were red from sleeping in my contacts; they were swollen and puffy from crying all night long. I felt empty...I felt alone...I felt numb. My soul hurt and my heart was broken.

You see, my younger brother, Tim passed away on April 21, 2017. Tim was not only my younger brother but also my best friend. Tim was the person I called when I needed advice, wanted to vent, or just wanted to laugh. The inside jokes and stories we shared were endless. We could be transparent with each other, without judgment. When I felt misunderstood by family, Tim was often my buffer.

While this was not my first experience with death, Tim's death shook my faith to the core. Why? I could not wrap my head around why God would allow this to happen to me, my mom, or my family.

Why would God do this? Why would God take two siblings within a 28-month span? In my mind, Tim was supposed to live; my family had done all the things in the natural we were supposed to do. We prayed on Tim's liver transplant as a family, and he was next in line on the transplant list. Everything we prayed and fasted for was falling into place. I visited him the week before he passed and planned to return after his transplant. We were raised in the church and my faith was unshakable, or so I thought.

Why would God do this? I was angry. After Tim's passing, I was angry at myself and felt guilty because I was not there when he passed. I was angry at Tim for giving up; he told me he was tired the year before, but I thought he was just having a moment. I was angry at God for taking my brother too soon. I did not know how to deal with those negative emotions. I felt confused, overwhelmed, and ashamed to admit my feelings.

As I think back over the last couple of years, I realized that I had experienced trauma from dysfunctional relationships that left a residue in my heart and led up to my emotional breakdown after Tim's passing. The first was a divorce from my cheating ex-husband. The second was an emotionally abusive relationship. Even though I walked away from these two situations, they both left me feeling lost, betrayed, bamboozled, and honestly, broken. However, as mothers do, I kept it moving and made sure my two daughters did not see me weakened or broken. I just faked it and masked my pain so that no one would notice how damaged I really was.

The third triggering event, which contributed to me hitting rock bottom, was a childhood sexual trauma that resurfaced from a conversation with my mother that left me feeling like I had just awakened from a nightmare. My coping mechanisms of avoidance and compartmentalizing trauma no longer worked.

Let's go back to Tim's passing in 2017, where my downward spiral continued. I could not get back up and as hard as I tried, I could not bounce back. As a result of those earlier unresolved traumas, I became depressed and suffered from anxiety and PTSD. This resulted in isolation from family and close friends. Despite attempts to function and act like everything was normal, things were far from normal, and I could no longer fake it. I didn't have a desire to get dressed, to be sociable, or even pray. My negative thoughts and emotions took over. Many days I would lie in bed, crying, and asking God to take away the pain and heal my heart. I felt like no one cared if I lived or died. I felt worthless and contemplated taking my own life. However, I knew if I committed suicide, I would go to hell, hurt my daughters, and leave them without a mother.

After several weeks of being in this negative place of despair, I finally decided to go back to my church and that day saved my life. While hesitantly participating in praise and worship, I silently whispered "God help me, I don't know what to do anymore. I need you, God." As I whispered those words, tears began to uncontrollably stream down my face. I raised my hands in worship and continued to cry throughout the service. At the end of service, I repented and felt a shift within my heart and spirit. However, the work did not stop there with church. God says in His Word, "...faith without works is dead." James 2:26. So, although I had taken the first step with getting my heart right with God, I knew there was a deeper work that needed to be done to get me out of that dark place. I reached out to a counselor and began intense, ongoing counseling for a period to support me properly in my grief and healing from past traumas.

As a result of my faith and my willingness and obedience to act on God's Word, I ultimately healed from my grief and my emotional traumas. I know my faith was shaken, but never lost. It says in God's Word, Matthew 17:20, NIV, He replied, "Because you have so little faith. Truly I tell you, if you have faith as small as a mustard seed, you can say to this mountain, 'Move from here to there,' and it will move. and Nothing will be impossible for you." I thank God for moving the mountains and for never leaving me.

QUESTIONS TO PONDER

1.What trauma do you need to take to the Lord for your healing?

2.In what areas of your life would you benefit from seeking wise counsel?

3.What is blocking you from emotional freedom?

UNSHAKABLE FAITH TO BECOME THE BEST VERSION OF YOURSELF

Mireille Toulekima

Award-winning global entrepreneur, Global Adviser in Energy and STEM, Public Figure, Global Influencer

ABOUT THE AUTHOR

Mireille Toulekima is a multi-talented woman whose versatility and accomplishments across diverse disciplines have earned her global recognition.

Mireille is an Award-winning global entrepreneur, Global Adviser in Energy and STEM, Public Figure, Global Influencer, Women empowerment advocate and champion, international speaker, published author and online talk show host. A petroleum engineer who gained her experience working for 25 years in Africa, Europe, Asia, and Australia in a range of technical and leadership roles for major oil, gas, energy, and STEM companies. This global touch is visible in her entrepreneurial ventures; her engineering career, leadership and coaching, publishing, and other related endeavours she actively engages.

Aside from her current role as a top-notch executive and partner to several global ventures and organizations, Mireille passionately participates with the class of women who have embraced non-traditional industries, globalization, innovation, and digital disruption as well as philanthropy, spiritual consciousness, and mindfulness.

Mireille is Managing Director of Perth Australia based MT Energy Resources, Limited. She also founded the

STEM Queens social venture to reach out and sponsor African and Indigenous Australian girls and women to embrace STEM and increase women participation in STEM sectors. In addition, she is the Global Chair – Engineering of the eminent and prestigious G100 Club and she hosts the global talk show, The Greatness Engineering hour show.

Mireille is part of the new waves of women who have embraced authentic leadership, non-traditional industries, globalization, innovation, and digital disruption.

My motto: DON'T LEAVE ANYTHING ON THE TABLE OF LIFE

Connect with Mireille:

- mireille.toulekima@toulekimaglobal.org
- Facebook Page: https://www.facebook.com/mireilletoulekimaglobal/
- LinkedIn: https://www.linkedin.com/in/mireille-toulekima
- Instagram: https://www.instagram.com/mireillemt/
- Twitter: @MTOULEKIMA

UNSHAKABLE FAITH TO BECOME THE BEST VERSION OF YOURSELF

I believe in greatness for all. We all have seeds of greatness within us. For me, success is the result of the faith we have in God and our personal beliefs. Our beliefs create our reality. Our estimation of our greatness and how we truly live it depends entirely on our faith and the framework of our personal beliefs. Our faith and beliefs provide a structured process through which we evaluate everything in our lives. If we want to have an outstanding life, it is imperative to have an unshakable faith in God and His ability to support and guide us in any circumstances along with His love for us, unconditionally. We must believe that we truly are the steering wheel of our lives under the guidance of God.

When we have unshakable faith and believe in God's promises, we become citizens of Heaven; the principles of God's Kingdom have power over earthly principles. We are set to withstand anything and achieve everything we set our mind to. And as rightly said by Dwight D. Eisenhower: "United in this determination and with unshakable faith in the cause for which we fight, we will, with God's help, go forward to our greatest victory."

There are victories to be won when we have unshakable faith. Dreams come true when we have unshakable faith.

The impossible becomes possible when we have unshakable faith. However, we must remember that unshakable faith must be first shaken before becoming unshakable. The faith that can't be shaken is the faith that has been shaken. Those circumstances in life that shake our world serve to build our faith.

Unshakable faith has carried me all the way from the best kept secret to being a global influencer who inspires and disrupts the world. You see, I come from a very humble beginning. The most valuable gift I had was the belief that God was guiding me all the way. Despite the challenges and obstacles, I have encountered, I've never doubted that God had a plan for me and that He gave me special gifts to help me attain greatness and become the best version of myself. This unshakable faith has carried me through when I lost my dad twenty-seven years ago and had to face one of the worse times of my life. In pain, broken and without any financial support, that's when things shifted for me. It is at this low point in my life that I was, in a way, directed to start a career in the energy sector. Out of necessity and desperation, I had to leave school and find a job to sustain both myself and my family financially. Little did I know that God was looking after me and was pushing me to create a trail where there was none. He was not only preparing me to step into my greatness but also to engineer greatness in the world. He drew me closer to Him through this tragedy and made me understand His power in my life. Through losing the person I loved so much and who counted the most in my life, God showed me that He was the only one who could heal me and give me back my joy and happiness. He led me to this unshakable faith that transcends any limitations. He taught me to be grateful to what happened and to give thanks in all circumstances. He taught me to always look for the best in everything and everyone and to be grateful for it. He taught me how to have this unshakable faith in myself to become everything I wanted to be. He taught me that I am unlimited and that any noticeable limitations were the limits I put on myself. He led me to learn from Abraham and adopt the key positive points of His leadership.

I was inspired by the story of Abraham in the Bible during my healing process after I lost my dad. I found that the story of Abraham in the Bible is very powerful for me and anyone who wants to have a true relationship with God and trusting Him, unconditionally. I understand that Abraham is our example for trusting God and that we are to respond the right way, in full obedience to God when we are tested. In that way, Abraham is a foreshadowed type of Jesus Christ and the ultimate example of what we can expect if we have faith and trust God unconditionally. Abraham stood out in his life as a man who sought God, who listened to God and who was eventually blessed by God. This was "revelation time" for me!!

In this VUCA (Volatile Uncertain Complex Ambiguous) world we live in and the shaky times resulting from it, everybody needs unshakable faith. We must emulate Abraham. Even when there was no reason for hope, Abraham kept hoping. He was fully convinced that God was able to do whatever He promised.

So, arm yourself with unshakable faith, believe and stand, regardless of circumstances or contrary evidence. God will guide you along the best pathway for your life. He will advise you and watch over you and often, with you not realizing it. Reviewing the passages in 2 Corinthians 5:1-10 reminds us that we are all people of unshakable faith. Unshakable faith allows us to see our lives and our world differently. Although we see present day loss, we consider our future hope. We see present day life having eternal ramifications.

It is time for us to step into the power that God makes available to us free of charge. Let's trust and believe in the promises He has for us. Let's harbour the unshakable faith that transcends all which will lead us to our greatness and to our best life.

We must build our lives on a strong foundation, on the kind of faith that won't be swayed with every wind of doctrine. Faith that will stand strong during a storm. Faith that may bend but refuses to break. The kind of faith that provokes God to unleash exponential favour upon our lives and uplift us to become unstoppable.

LOVE LIKE YOU'VE NEVER BEEN HURT

Evangelist Bertha D. Winston

Radio Personality on 1340 AM WYCB
Owner of Destined2Millions and the Winston Experience Financial Success Companies
Mary Kay Consultant, and co-owner of The Pavilion Event and Conference Center

ABOUT THE AUTHOR

Evangelist Bertha D. Winston is a Radio Personality where she hosted the Eagle Kind Radio Broadcast on 1340 AM WYCB for the last seven years. She is the oldest of eleven children, and she is a loving wife to Clifton H. Winston, Jr. of 52 years. She is the proud mother of three adult children: two daughters and one son, six grandchildren and two great grandchildren.

Evangelist Bertha Winston has been a member of Jesus Way Temple Christian Church for 40 plus years. She serves as Secretary, Board Member, Worship Leader and as an Associate Minister.

She is also a board member for the foreign missions in the Republic of Haiti. She served as board member and several other offices for the National Network for Christian Men and Women. She is the Office Manager for a prestigious law firm in the DMV metropolitan area. She is an entrepreneur, and she owns several businesses.

Love Like You've Never Been Hurt

"Love suffers long and is kind; love does not envy; love does not parade itself, is not [a]puffed up; 5 does not behave rudely, does not seek its own, is not provoked, [b]thinks no evil; 6 does not rejoice in iniquity, but rejoices in the truth; 7 bears all things, believes all things, hopes all things, endures all things." 1 Corinthians 13: 4-7

I was born in Franklin, Virginia. I am the proud mother of three children: one son and two daughters, six grandchildren and two great grandchildren.

I am an entrepreneur, co-owner of the Pavilion Exclusive Event and Conference Center, a board member for Haiti Mission as well as for my Church, Jesus Way Temple Christian Church; I have been an Evangelist and associate minister for my church for over 40 years. Currently, I am an office manager for a prestigious law firm.

I am blessed to share that I have developed an exemplary professional career in which my desire was to educate and inspire women to become more knowledgeable about their financial freedom through Destined2Millions and through the Winston Experience.

I grew up as a foster child in Jackson, North Carolina.

Unfortunately, my foster mother died when I was five years old. After her death, I was shifted from one foster sister and brother to the other. During the time I was living with one of my foster sisters in Norfolk, Virginia, and unfortunately, I was mistreated, abused taken advantage of, as well as experiencing the horrible pain of molestation, and other horrific situations. My foster sister ended up being arrested for child abuse. I did not understand why I was treated so badly by her, but I found out later that she hated my mother, so she took it out on me. I was a very lonely and unhappy child, who almost never smiled. I thought life was useless because my life was so miserable, so consequently, I hated my life. I prayed to die many times. But God had a specific plan for my life. See Jeremiah 29:11: "For I know the thoughts that I think toward you, says the Lord, thoughts of peace and not of evil, to give you a future and a hope." At age 14, my other foster sister moved me to Washington, D.C. to live with her and to assist her with her daughter. I thought this would be the beginning of a good experience for me and a new start for me, until my foster brother started taking advantage of me. He would take pleasure in molesting me at every opportunity when he found me home alone. Of course, I was afraid to tell anyone because I was threatened by him, and he convinced me that no one would believe me anyway. I had read and heard of many stories of this same horrific situation happening to many innocent young girls, so I know it to be true because I was a victim. You cannot help but ponder these horrendous acts in your heart and ask God, "Why and how could He allow such a hurtful thing to happen to an innocent young girl. Life seemed useless when you are being taken advantage of by a person who is supposed to love and protect you and not take advantage of you. When traumas like this happen to you, your trust is very limited; you feel dirty, sad, lonely violated, and one can experience suicidal tendencies, and you think that your life will never amount to anything. All kinds of sad, bad, negative thoughts wander through your mind, BUT God! He indeed is a keeper, a sustainer, a deliverer, and He does watch over the innocent.

I realized later in life that pain and suffering does not last forever if you have faith in God. At the age of 16 I had a baby out of wedlock. This was not something I planned nor was I prepared for, but it happened. I was still in high school, working a job and taking care of a newborn. I eventually moved out of my foster sister's home and moved in with one of my foster brothers and his family. Take one guess at which foster brother that was. At age 17, I was hired to work at a hospital, trying to make the best life for me and my daughter, so in 1968, I started working at Sibley Memorial Hospital where I met the love of my life, Clifton H. Winston, Jr. We started dating in November 1968 and we were married in April 1969 (6 months later) which was one month before my high school graduation, and we have been married for 52 years now. This was the beginning of a happy life for me. He taught me how to love and be loved. He taught me how to appreciate myself and he promised me that I would never have to worry about being mistreated / misused and taken advantage of ever again, because he was going to take care of me for the rest of my life. He was raised in a home with a loving mother and father who manifested love daily, and that was very important for me to witness. You see, God knows how to put the right people together. What if I had married someone who had the same low self-esteem I possessed and was raised in a home with the same kind of abuse I experienced; we would not have been very compatible.

In 1975 my husband decided this would be a good time to pack up his family from DC and move to a new location to start a new life in Maryland. My heart, mind and soul were at peace, and by this time, I was ready to start a new career. I was offered a job at the Board of Education in Prince George's County, Maryland as an Administrative Assistant and I was very excited about starting a new job. Shortly after working at the Board of Education, I was diagnosed with that awful word no one ever wants to hear– Cancer. Talk about not having faith, hearing news of this sort, is a time that if you don't know God –you had better get acquainted with Him and get acquainted with Him quick. After much prayer and seeking God, I decided I would not go through chemo or radiation, so I had a Mastectomy on my right breast. I am so proud to say that I have been a cancer survivor for 13 years now. To God be all the glory for the great things He has done in my life! Soon I will be retiring from my job of 13 years at age 71. My advice to you is to never give up hope and keep the faith. God will see you through every trial and tribulation.

MY UNSHAKABLE VISION

Minister ALLISON G. DANIELS

Founder, Allison Daniels Ministries, LLC
Founder/CEO of AGD Publishing Services, LLC
Founder/CEO of the Write 2 Finish Now! Book Program
Founder/CEO of Women Empowered 2 Win Organization
Monday Morning Facebook Live @ 5 am Segment/ The Authors Lab Podcast

ABOUT THE VISIONARY AUTHOR

As an Awarding-Winning, 4x Best-selling author who has written over 31 books and a Life Coach, I have been extremely honored and blessed to help empower women in various stages of their lives, who are seeking professional and personal growth through venues that provide motivation, awareness, and mentoring.

Allison teaches life skills to women in the form of discipleship, stewardship and servant leadership via networking, teaching, mentoring, workshops, conferences, and the like. She is the owner of Allison Daniels Ministries, LLC; Founder/CEO of the Write 2 Finish Now! Book Program where she teaches writers how to write their books and share their stories. She is the Founder/CEO of AGD Publishing Services, where it is her mission to turn writers into success authors –one book at a time.

She is the Founder/CEO of Women Empowered 2 Win Organization, which is geared to empower and educate women of all ages to lead with authority. She is an accomplished Author, Speaker, Coach, and Licensed Minister.

Also, Allison has a Monday Morning Facebook Live @ 5am Segment, and she is a former Contributing Co-Host of the WBGR radio show "LetsDoThis". She is the Host of two (2) Podcasts – Authors Chat with Allison and The Authors Lab. She uses her books, coaching and her mentoring skills as tools to help and assist those who are ready to lead with authority, lead with clarity and lead with confidence toward their next level up. Her mission is to Aspire, Dream and Motivate others. Allison was both enlightened and inspired when she read "Re-discovering Faith: Understanding the Nature of Kingdom Living", where Dr. Myles Munroe strips away misconceptions surrounding faith and reveals the nature, character, and power of true faith.

MY UNSHAKABLE VISION

And the LORD answered me: "Write the vision; make it plain on tablets, so he may run who reads it. Habakkuk 2:2 KJV

In January 2019 we had a major snowstorm in the DMV area, and I was told that I needed to come to work that very next day. But anyone that knew me understood that I didn't drive in snow and very heavy rain. So, I prayed that God would allow us one more day to be at home so that the streets could be cleared off. Well, my prayer was answered. But, when I woke up that morning I cried out to God and I said, "God, I cannot, and I will not allow someone else to constantly dictate to me how to handle the safeness for me taking care of myself.

So, I woke up at 3:30am that following morning and I sent out over 50 Emails to every television staff member I could think of who would interview me and allow me to share my story about my Book, "Walk in Your Authority" (Unleashing the Divine Power from Within) and my upcoming book, Empowered to Win (which was published in 2021).

Well, at 5:30am that same day, I received an email from News Channel 7, inviting me to be a guest on their show. The five topics I provided to them were all favorable topics but the one we settle on was, "From Fear to Freedom" and wouldn't you know it I came into the studio on the same day we celebrated Martin Luther King, Jr. Holiday.

Then, in August 2019 I was pondering over a future decision I had to make. When I read the above Scripture, it stood out, in fact, it impacted me greatly because I knew that God was speaking directly to me, because I was pondering on whether or not I should start my publishing company during the pandemic.

What is the definition of VISION? A vision is something seen in a dream, trance, or religious ecstasy, especially a supernatural appearance that usually conveys a revelation. Visions generally have more clarity than dreams. Most of us have a vision of how we want our story to be told or how our story should be shared about our lives.

In August 2019, as a 4x Best-selling, International Author and VISIONARY Author of the Book Empowered to Win, 2nd Edition Anthology, my vision was manifested; I started my publishing company, AGD Publishing Services, where it is my mission to turn writers into successful authors, one book at a time.

HELPFUL POINTERS

1.You must write your vision out.

2.You must speak life changing words.

3.You must stop looking back at your past.

QUOTE FROM MY PREVIOUS BOOK, EMPOWERED TO WIN:

You are Empowered to WRITE Now! The Word of God says, "Where there is no vision, the people perish: but he that keepeth the law, happy is he." Proverbs 29:18 (KJV) So, I ask you, do you have a vision to see your book written –to have your story told and to take back your voice and your life?

QUESTIONS FOR YOU TO ANSWER:

Write out 2 of your weaknesses, and how you plan to improve on them:

1.

2.

Write out 2 of your strengths and meditate on them:

1.

2.

MY UNSHAKABLE VISION

"No weapon that is formed against thee shall prosper; and every tongue that shall rise against thee in judgment thou shalt condemn. This is the heritage of the servants of the LORD, and their righteousness is of me, saith the LORD." Isaiah 54:17 (KJV)

BIBLICAL SOURCES

Are You Ready (Finally) to Write Your Story?

Now is the time for you to share your story. Now is the time to put pen/paper together (or type) your thoughts, just as God has already given you. Just like these bold and courageous women are sharing their truth; it's time for you to break the cycle, break the silence and WRITE YOUR OWN TRUTH!!!

Speak Your Truth Because Your Story MATTERS!

Are you finally ready to be bold, strong, write, share, and publish your truth, so that you will be a blessing to others? This will encourage others to do the same; healing will take place in so many areas of your life!

If you believe that this is your time, and you are ready to share your story, and you want more information about how you can be an author or a co-author email allisongdaniels@verizon.net OR visit allisongdaniels.com.

Allison G. Daniels
Visionary, Empowered to Win!

BOOKS PUBLISHED BY AGD PUBLISHING

CEO/FOUNDER
ALLISON G. DANIELS

Empowered to Win, 2nd Edition Anthology
Allison G. Daniels, Visionary, 2021

Spiritual Mindset
Pastor Daniel T. Mangrum, 2020

Exposing Shame
Co-Pastor Sabrina A. Mangrum, 2020

Pressing Forward
Bishop Mary E. Adams, 2020

Breakthrough: Book of Poems and Prayers
Felicia Edmond, 2020

Published Books by Allison G. Daniels

Untold Feelings of a Poet (1993–2012)

Private Fears That No One Else Hears (1995–2012)

Beyond Hope (1996–2012)

Yearning for Love (1996–2006)

Jesus A Joy to Call My Own (1996–2006)

Black Man I Love You (1997–2005)

Revitalizing Your Spirit (1998–2005)

A Glimpse of Glory (1998–2005)

Sweet Memories of Yesterday (1996–2006)

I Dream in Colors (1998–2005)

Facing Tomorrow (2000)

Taking Back My Life (2002–2005)

Comfort Corner (2003–2006)

Changing Winds (2003–2006)

Love Expressed through A Poet (2003–2005)

Mother I Love You (2003)

Poems for all Occasions (2004–2007)

Books Authored by Allison G. Daniels

A Tribute to President Obama (2010–2011)

A Tribute to Whitney Houston (2012)

The Spirit of a Woman (2011–2012)

Life Goes On (2013)

Happy Valentine Day with Love (2012)

Daily Words of Wisdom (2012)

How to Self-Publish a Book (2014)

Pink Side of Me (2014)

Quotes of Wisdom (2012)

Poems for all Occasions II (2012)

When I Did When My Loved

Passed Away (2013)

Love Poems (2014)

Tribute to President, Barak Obama (2014)

*Walk in Your Authority *Unleash the Divine*

Power from Within (2016)

CO-AUTHORED BY ALLISON G. DANIELS

How to Survive When Your Ship is Sinking (2012)

Releasing Strongholds (2012)

Teenage Girls (2014)

The Female Leader (2012)

Celebration of Life (2012)

Bully Me No More (2013)

Coaching Guru Nook II (2015)

Sharing Our Prayers (2018)

Writing is Essential (2019)

Book Coach/Consultant

ALLISON G. DANIELS

Broken Peace by Kristian Gregory-Lee

I Believe I Can Fly by Jackie Petty

Behind the Chair by Alice (Doll)

Made in the USA
Columbia, SC
24 September 2022

67481668R10087